ASSESSMENT OF THE LEGAL STATUS OF SEXUAL AND GENDER MINORITIES IN 17 COUNTRIES IN ASIA AND THE PACIFIC

MAY 2024

ASIAN DEVELOPMENT BANK

ADB

© 2024 Asian Development Bank
6 ADB Avenue, Mandaluyong City, 1550 Metro Manila, Philippines
Tel +63 2 8632 4444; Fax +63 2 8636 2444
www.adb.org

Some rights reserved. Published in 2024.

ISBN 978-92-9270-718-7 (print); 978-92-9270-719-4 (PDF); 978-92-9270-720-0 (ebook)
Publication Stock No. SPR240285-2
DOI: http://dx.doi.org/10.22617/SPR240285-2

The views expressed in this publication are those of the authors and do not necessarily reflect the views and policies of the Asian Development Bank (ADB) or its Board of Governors or the governments they represent.

ADB does not guarantee the accuracy of the data included in this publication and accepts no responsibility for any consequence of their use. The mention of specific companies or products of manufacturers does not imply that they are endorsed or recommended by ADB in preference to others of a similar nature that are not mentioned.

By making any designation of or reference to a particular territory or geographic area in this document, ADB does not intend to make any judgments as to the legal or other status of any territory or area.

Corrigenda to ADB publications may be found at http://www.adb.org/publications/corrigenda.

Notes:
In this publication, "$" refers to United States dollars.
ADB recognizes "China" as the People's Republic of China; "Hong Kong" as Hong Kong, China; "Korea" and "South Korea" as the Republic of Korea; "Kyrgyzstan" as the Kyrgyz Republic; and "Vietnam" as Viet Nam.

Cover design by Mike Cortes, using images (from left) Romanchini/Shutterstock, Ranta Images/Shutterstock, SFIO CRACHO/Shutterstock, Roman Samborskyi/Shutterstock, 2p2play/Shutterstock, project1photography/Shutterstock, Daxiao Productions/Shutterstock, Nozim Kalandarov/ADB, Daxiao Productions/Shutterstock, Abir Abdullah/ADB, fizkes/Shutterstock, Daxiao Productions/Shutterstock, Chay_Tee/Shutterstock, Makistock/Shutterstock, and Mangostar/Shutterstock.

CONTENTS

TABLES, FIGURES, AND BOXES

FOREWORD

At the Asian Development Bank (ADB), we are committed to upholding the principles of diversity, equity, and inclusion in all aspects of our institution and operations. This commitment aligns closely with our core values and strategic objectives, reflecting our dedication to supporting positive change and advocating greater inclusivity within our workplace and beyond. Recognizing the importance of social inclusion, encompassing sexual orientation, gender identity, expression, and sex characteristics (SOGIESC), ADB undertook a study of the legal frameworks affecting people with diverse SOGIESC and of legal challenges to their recognition, empowerment, and inclusion across various domains. The objective was to create an evidence-based reference for use in identifying potential areas for legal reform assistance, to be explored and discussed with partners in our member countries.

The report presents the findings of the study. It aims to expand the knowledge base on this critical and emerging development issue by presenting data and information on the stigmas and discrimination sexual and gender minorities face as a result of existing laws. With this goal in mind, this initiative aims to strengthen evidence-based inclusive policy dialogue on legal reform areas, offering policy recommendations adaptable to member countries' aspirations and sociocultural values. The report offers a range of options for governments and ADB regarding identifying entry points for transformative support in policy dialogue, legal reform, and operational responses, by facilitating the sharing and cross-fertilization of emerging practices in Asia and the Pacific.

Fatima Yasmin
Vice-President
Sectors and Themes
Asian Development Bank

PREFACE

This report gives the Asian Development Bank (ADB) a better understanding of the critical legal barriers to recognizing diverse sexual orientation, gender identity and expression, and sex characteristics (SOGIESC) in select countries in the Asia and Pacific region. This understanding represents a crucial step toward our identifying possible areas of assistance in policy reform to combat the long-standing exclusion and discrimination this segment of society experiences. I am pleased that we have taken this step.

Following the World Bank's *Equality of Opportunity for Sexual and Gender Minorities* study (2021) methodology, this report examines the systemic legal barriers hindering the realization of rights and freedoms for sexual and gender minorities in education, labor markets, public services, social protection, and civil and political inclusion. It provides better knowledge of modalities for ADB's engagement with governments in strengthening policy and legal frameworks for greater social inclusion impact in our operations.

The study results show significant disparities in legal protections across the countries in Asia and the Pacific, with varying levels of decriminalization and safeguards against discrimination based on SOGIESC. This is compounded by a lack of legal gender recognition. An absence of national action plans and human rights institutions hinders civil and political inclusion efforts. In addition, a lack of legislation against conversion therapy and nonconsensual surgeries on intersex children underscores the need for comprehensive legal reforms. Urgent action is needed to address hate crimes targeting sexual and gender minorities, including training for law enforcement and the provision of support services.

I sincerely thank all contributors, including our dedicated team of researchers, legal experts, and community partners, with special appreciation to Francesco Tornieri. Collaboration between ADB and the World Bank produced the *Assessment of the Legal Status of Sexual and Gender Minorities in 17 Countries in Asia and the Pacific.*

As you explore this publication, I encourage you to reflect on potential modalities to engage with our clients in furthering SOGIESC inclusion. Let us continue striving for a world where inclusion and diversity are celebrated, and where every person is treated with the dignity and respect they deserve.

Ramesh Subramanian
Director General and Chief
Sectors Group
Asian Development Bank

ACKNOWLEDGMENTS

The Asian Development Bank (ADB) developed this *Assessment of the Legal Status of Sexual and Gender Minorities in 17 Countries in Asia and the Pacific* in collaboration with the World Bank. The report follows an established methodology of the World Bank's *Equality of Opportunity for Sexual and Gender Minorities* (EQOSOGI) report.

Samreen Shahbaz authored the report and oversaw the research process. The core research team comprised Samreen Shahbaz, Lucia Arnal Rodriguez, Dariga Chukmaitova, and Benjie D. Zabala, along with two technical resource persons from the World Bank—Christian De la Medina Soto and John Arzinos—who provided technical input and quality assurance during data collection phases of the research.

Francesco Tornieri, principal social development specialist (social inclusion), Human and Social Development Sector Office, Sectors Group, ADB, provided comprehensive guidance on developing the report and analyzing the data following the initial work of Oliver Chapman, former senior social development specialist, then NGO and Civil Society Center, ADB.

The development of the report benefited significantly from the expertise of a team of country experts and legal experts from both within and outside ADB, as well as members of regional lesbian, gay, bisexual, transgender, and intersex groups. The report team acknowledges and extends gratitude to all individuals and organizations that provided technical review and substantive contributions to the report: Holning Lau, Willie P. Mangum, distinguished professor of Law at the University of North Carolina School of Law; Andrew Park, senior advisor on Inclusive Development at Outright International; Ajita Banerjie, senior program officer at the International Lesbian, Gay, Bisexual, Trans and Intersex Association Asia; Ryan Joseph Figueiredo, executive director of the Equal Asia Foundation; Ryan Silverio of the Association of Southeast Asian Nations Sexual Orientation, Gender Identity and Expression Caucus; Timo T. Ojanen of Thammasat University; Nada Chaiyajit and Abhina Aher of the Asia Pacific Coalition on Male Sexual Health; Kathryn Johnson, policy specialist in the HIV and Health Group at the Bangkok Regional Hub of the United Nations Development Programme; Nadira Masiumova of the Eurasian Coalition on Male Health; and Brenda Batistiana, senior social development (social inclusion) consultant, ADB.

The report team also expresses gratitude for the thought leadership and input provided by Clifton Cortez, sexual orientation and gender identity global advisor with Operations Policy and Country Services, and Julia Constanze Braunmiller, senior private sector development specialist, both at the World Bank.

ABBREVIATIONS

ADB	–	Asian Development Bank
APTN	–	Asia Pacific Transgender Network
ART	–	assisted reproductive technology
CCMD	–	Chinese Classification of Mental Disorders
CSO	–	civil society organizations
DMC	–	developing member country
EQOSOGI	–	Equality of Opportunity for Sexual and Gender Minorities
GDP	–	gross domestic product
GILRHO	–	Global Index on Legal Recognition of Homosexual Orientation
GNP+	–	Global Network of People Living with HIV
ICD-11	–	International Classification of Diseases, 11th Revision
ILO	–	International Labour Organization
IVF	–	in-vitro fertilization
MSM	–	men who have sex with men
LGBTI	–	lesbian, gay, bisexual, transgender, and intersex
SOGI	–	sexual orientation and gender identity
SOGIE	–	sexual orientation, gender identity and expression
SOGIESC	–	sexual orientation, gender identity and expression, and sex characteristics
TRI	–	Transgender Rights Index
UNDP	–	United Nations Development Programme
UNESCO	–	United Nations Educational, Scientific and Cultural Organization
USAID	–	United States Agency for International Development
WHO	–	World Health Organizaion

GLOSSARY

This section provides a list of terminologies to build a shared understanding of concepts related to sexual orientation, gender identity and expressions, and sex characteristics (SOGIESC). The section captures these concepts and terminologies in English and does not encompass cultural and indigenous terms related to "sexual orientation" and "gender identity;" therefore, this list is not exhaustive.

Assisted reproductive technology. Describes all treatments or procedures for reproduction, including in-vitro management of both human oocytes and sperm or embryos. These treatments include but are not limited to in-vitro fertilization, embryo transfer, and gestational surrogacy. Assisted reproductive technology (ART) does not include sperm donation (based on International Committee for Monitoring Assisted Reproductive Technology and World Health Organization. 2009. Revised Glossary on ART Terminology).

Cisgender. Refers to a person whose gender identity corresponds with the sex registered at birth.

Conversion therapy. Used as an umbrella term to describe a diverse range of procedures that aim to change a homosexual person's sexual orientation to heterosexual or a transgender or gender-diverse person's gender identity to cisgender. "Conversion therapy" practices are harmful interventions that are rooted in the false belief that a person's sexual orientation or gender identity can be changed through medical, psychological, or faith-based interventions (based on the United Nations Independent Expert on Sexual Orientation and Gender Identity (SOGI). 2020. Practices of So-Called Conversion Therapies. Geneva).

Discrimination. Multiple and intersecting direct or indirect unequal or unfair treatment, which is based on one or more grounds, such as a person's age; sexual orientation, gender identity and expression, and sex characteristics (SOGIESC); race; ethnicity; and religion.

Gender-affirming health care. Refers to any form of health care that trans and nonbinary people receive to affirm their gender identity when it is not aligned with their sex assigned at birth. It can include nonmedical and medical care, such as gender-affirming hormone therapy and a wide range of gender-affirming surgeries (based on World Professional Association for Transgender Health. 2021. Standard of Care. Version 8).

Gender dysphoria. Refers to the emotional and mental stress a person feels due to a mismatch between their gender identity and their sex assigned at birth (based on World Professional Association for Transgender Health. 2021. Standard of Care. Version 8).

Gender expression. Refers to each person's expression of their gender through physical appearance—including dress, hairstyle, mannerisms, speech, names, and personal pronouns. Gender expression may or may not conform to a person's gender identity.

Gender identity. Refers to a person's deeply felt internal and individual experience of gender (e.g., being a man, a woman, neither, or something else), which may or may not correspond with their sex assigned at birth or the gender attributed to them by society. It includes the personal sense of the body (which may involve, if freely chosen, modification of appearance or function by medical, surgical, or other means) and expressions of gender, including dress, speech, and mannerisms. Gender identity is not synonymous with sexual orientation. Gender identity is internal and is not necessarily visible to others (based on J. Arzinos, C. Medina Soto, and C. Cortez. 2021. *Equality of Opportunity for Sexual and Gender Minorities*. Washington, DC: World Bank).

Gender markers. A gender marker represents an individual's gender identity in official documents, such as IDs, passports, etc. Commonly used gender markers are F (female), M (male), and X or Other (intersex, nonbinary, gender nonconfirming, transgender).

Hate crimes. Offenses that are motivated by prejudice or bias against a particular group of people. This prejudice could be based on ethnicity, religion, sexual orientation, gender identity and expression, or sex characteristics. Hate crime laws are typified in two ways: (i) through substantive hate crime laws, such as laws that include biased motive of the crimes as an integral part of the offense; and (ii) through penalty enhancement laws, for example as an "aggravating circumstance," e.g., heightened punishment for an offense when committed with a biased motive (based on J. Arzinos, C. Medina Soto, and C. Cortez. 2021. *Equality of Opportunity for Sexual and Gender Minorities*. Washington, DC: World Bank).

Homophobia, transphobia, biphobia, intersex-phobia. The fear, hatred, or intolerance of homosexual people (homophobia), trans people (transphobia), bisexual people (biphobia), and intersex people (intersex-phobia). These terms also describe discrimination based on sexual orientation, gender identity and expression, and sex characteristics.

Intersex. An umbrella term for people who are born with one or more variations in biological sex characteristics that fall outside the typical conception of male or female bodies. These characteristics could include hormonal patterns, chromosomes, and sexual anatomy. Intersex characteristics can be identified at birth; in other cases, people may not discover their intersex traits until puberty or later in life (based on OHCHR. 2023. *Technical Note on the Human Rights of Intersex People: Human Rights Standards and Good Practices*. Geneva).

Legal gender recognition. Refers to laws, regulations, and administrative procedures through which a person can change their legal gender marker and name on official identity documents (based on United Nations Independent Expert on SOGI. 2018. Legal Recognition of Gender Identity and Depathologization. Geneva).

Old-age benefits. May include periodic pensions, subsidized long-term care, and transportation allowances for older persons.

Pathologizing. Refers to the medical and legal practice of describing an attribute of an individual or a group of people as "intrinsically disordered." Medical professionals and authorities often categorize trans people as inherently pathological, therefore requiring them to seek psychological or medical interventions (based on United Nations Independent Expert on SOGI. 2018. Legal Recognition of Gender Identity and Depathologization. Geneva).

Pathologizing requirements. Transgender identity has been pathologized as a mental disorder or gender dysphoria in several countries across the world. In these country contexts, trans persons are required to undergo a medical diagnosis as a precondition to receiving gender-affirming hormonal treatment or surgeries. Pathologizing requirements discussed in this study refer to these diverse medical diagnosis conditions.

Sexual and gender minorities. Used to describe people whose sexual orientation, gender identity and expressions, and sex characteristics differ from those of heterosexual cisgender people. The term is often used for LGBTI people. Both "LGBTI" and "LGBTQI+" are inclusive terms used to represent a range of sexual orientations and gender identities, and the choice between them often depends on regional, cultural, or organizational preferences. For the purpose of this publication, LGBTI is being used to represent lesbian, gay, bisexual, transgender, and intersex individuals, recognizing diverse sexual orientations and gender identities.

Sexual orientation. Refers to heterosexuality, homosexuality, bisexuality, and a wide range of other expressions of sexual orientations. An individual's sexual orientation is characterized by one or more of the following: how a person identifies their sexual orientation, a person's capacity to experience sexual and/or romantic attraction to people of the same and/or different gender, and/or a person's sexual behavior with people of the same and/or different gender (based on Outright International. 2022. *"We Deserve Protection": Anti-LGBTIQ Legislation and Violence in Ghana.* New York: Outright International).

Sex characteristics. Refer to a range of biological features, including hormone patterns, chromosome patterns, sexual anatomy, and reproductive anatomy (based on J. Arzinos, C. Medina Soto, and C. Cortez. 2021. *Equality of Opportunity for Sexual and Gender Minorities.* Washington, DC: World Bank, and OHCHR. 2023. *Technical Note on the Human Rights of Intersex People: Human Rights Standards and Good Practices.* Geneva).

Social protection. A set of legal, regulatory, and policy interventions designed to reduce and prevent poverty and financial vulnerability of individual citizens or a population group. Social protection addresses financial vulnerability through a range of interventions, such as public health insurance, unemployment benefits, and social housing (based on J. Arzinos, C. Medina Soto, and C. Cortez. 2021. *Equality of Opportunity for Sexual and Gender Minorities.* Washington, DC: World Bank).

Social protection for low-income families with children. May include but is not limited to maternity allowances, tax benefits for low-income families, child benefits, and parental allowances for children's care (based on J. Arzinos, C. Medina Soto, and C. Cortez. 2021. *Equality of Opportunity for Sexual and Gender Minorities.* Washington, DC: World Bank).

Social protection for health care. May include but is not limited to subsidized public health insurance, public insurance programs for people over a certain age, and health care coverage for marginalized population groups (based on J. Arzinos, C. Medina Soto, and C. Cortez. 2021. *Equality of Opportunity for Sexual and Gender Minorities.* Washington, DC: World Bank).

Social protection for people with severe disability. May include initiatives by the government to provide allowances to persons who may be unable to work owing to the severity of their disability.

Social housing. May include, but is not limited to, government-owned public housing and caps or limits to rent increases (based on J. Arzinos, C. Medina Soto, and C. Cortez. 2021. *Equality of Opportunity for Sexual and Gender Minorities.* Washington, DC: World Bank).

Transgender. Transgender (or "trans") refers to individuals whose sex assigned at birth does not correspond to their gender identity. "Trans" is being used as an umbrella term, and it encompasses trans men, trans women, and other gender-diverse people.

Unemployment benefits. May include, but are not limited to, allowances and direct cash transfers for a determined period to unemployed individuals.

Vagrancy. Literally means the state of being homeless, jobless, and often moving from place to place without a fixed or permanent residence or means of support. In the context of this report, vagrancy refers to the definitions employed in the penal codes that are imported from or inspired by the 1824 Vagrancy Act in England.

EXECUTIVE SUMMARY

This study examines laws and regulations that promote the inclusion of sexual and gender minorities or people with diverse sexual orientation, gender identity and expression, and sex characteristics (SOGIESC) and discourage discrimination against them across a range of sectors, including **education**, **labor markets**, **public services**, **social protection**, and **civil and political inclusion**. It covers 17 countries: Armenia, Bhutan, Cambodia, Fiji, Georgia, the Kyrgyz Republic, Mongolia, Nepal, New Zealand, Papua New Guinea, the People's Republic of China, the Philippines, the Republic of Korea, Sri Lanka, Thailand, Timor-Leste, and Viet Nam. It also provides a mapping of laws that provide protections from SOGIESC-based hate crimes and conversion therapy practices, among other forms of violence against sexual and gender minorities. Further, the study offers recommendations to governments for legal and policy reforms to promote the inclusion of sexual and gender minorities and improve their development outcomes. The study follows an established methodology of the World Bank's study, *Equality of Opportunity for Sexual and Gender Minorities* (EQOSOGI), through the use of six indicator sets. Key findings from each indicator set are provided below:

1. **Decriminalization of sexual and gender minorities.** The majority of the countries analyzed have decriminalized consensual same-sex activity between consenting adults. However, the extent and level of protection for sexual and gender minorities differ across nations. Some countries have comprehensive antidiscrimination laws that protect lesbian, gay, bisexual, transgender, and intersex (LGBTI) individuals, whereas others—such as **Papua New Guinea** and **Sri Lanka**—have no legal protections in place, with same-sex activity between consenting adults criminalized. At the same time, two countries, **Nepal** and **Sri Lanka**, have enacted vagrancy and public nuisance-related laws that penalize and target LGBTI people, and at least half of the countries analyzed have criminalized the sexual conduct of people living with HIV.

2. **Access to education.** Of the 17 analyzed countries, six have some legal protections against SOGIESC-based discrimination in the education sector. For example, Fiji has provided constitutional protections against discrimination on the grounds of sexual orientation and gender identity and expression and has guaranteed the right to education for all. There are local ordinances and regulations in at least two countries, the **Philippines** and the **Republic of Korea**, prohibiting the victimization of LGBTI students. Further, there are antibullying and cyberbullying laws that extend protection against sexual orientation and gender identity-related bullying in educational settings in **New Zealand** and the **Philippines**. Within this indicator set, most of the positive developments are related to the inclusion of SOGIESC in the sexual education curriculum in a positive and inclusive manner. Legal protections for intersex persons are missing in the current legislative framework in all analyzed countries.

3. **Access to labor markets.** Of the 17 countries in the study sample, eight have enacted laws and regulations that provide some degree of protection against SOGIESC-based discrimination in the workplace. For example, **Mongolia** enacted the Revised Labor Code in 2021, which explicitly prohibits discrimination based on sexual orientation. The **Philippines** prohibits discrimination against LGBTI people applying for civil service examinations. Some examined countries have included explicit provisions against unfair dismissal and wage-related discrimination, such as **Fiji**, where the Employment Relations Act 2007 prohibits unfair dismissal and less favorable pay on the grounds of sexual orientation and gender identity and expression. However, very few countries have mechanisms to receive and investigate complaints of SOGIESC-related discrimination in the workplace. For example, **Thailand** has established the Committee on Consideration of Unfair Gender Discrimination (WorLorPor), mandated to receive and investigate complaints of gender identity-based discrimination across various sectors. Legal protections for intersex persons are missing in the current legislative framework in all analyzed countries.

4. **Access to public services and social protection.** Laws that guarantee nondiscrimination based on SOGIESC in access to public services (such as health care) and social protection (such as social housing and social protection for older people, people with disabilities, and low-income families) are nonexistent in the region. Even in contexts where enabling laws and regulations exist, such as the **Republic of Korea**, **Mongolia**, and **Nepal**, LGBTI people remain invisible. In other countries, the lack of legal gender recognition poses a structural barrier for transgender people to access health care and social protection.

5. **Civil and political inclusion.** Civil rights encompass personal liberties and protections from intrusion or infringement on individual freedoms, whereas political rights involve participation in the political process and having a voice in governance and decision-making. In most countries, there are no national action plans or national human rights institutions with a mandate to promote the civil and political inclusion or rights of sexual and gender minorities. **Except for Nepal**, most countries do not include sexual and gender minorities in the national census. Laws against conversion therapy practices are nonexistent in all analyzed countries **except New Zealand**. None of the analyzed countries have laws against nonemergency, nonconsensual surgeries on intersex children.

6. **Protection from hate crimes.** Laws that criminalize hate crimes against people with diverse SOGIESC are lacking in all analyzed countries except **Georgia** and **Mongolia**. Further, no laws and regulations mandate the training of law enforcement authorities and judicial personnel to recognize and manage cases of SOGIESC-based hate crimes in a sensitive way. At the same time, there are no laws or regulations in place to mandate the provision of support services, such as legal aid and shelter, to victims of SOGIESC-based hate crimes.

Findings from the 17 countries assessed in the Asian Development Bank's (ADB) study complement the data presented in the World Bank's EQOSOGI research initiative, which looked at good practices as well as lack of protection for sexual and gender minorities in Bangladesh, India, and Indonesia. The varying degrees of protections provided by the laws and regulations of countries assessed in ADB and World Bank studies are presented in the figure:

Figure: Overview of the Status of Legal Inclusion of Sexual and Gender Minorities

A. World Bank Study (2021)

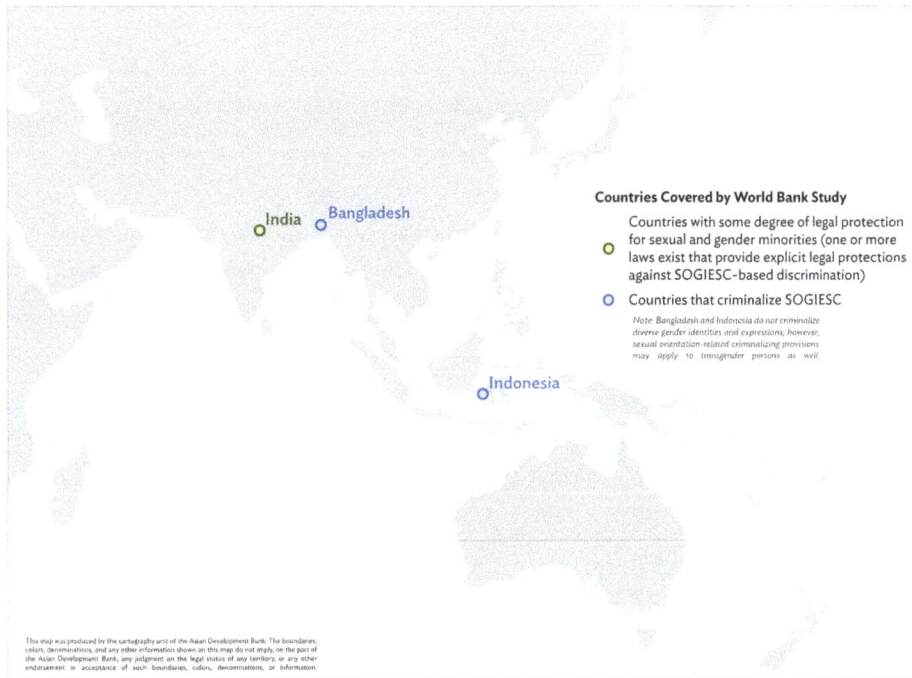

Countries Covered by World Bank Study

○ (green) Countries with some degree of legal protection for sexual and gender minorities (one or more laws exist that provide explicit legal protections against SOGIESC-based discrimination)

○ (blue) Countries that criminalize SOGIESC

Note: Bangladesh and Indonesia do not criminalize diverse gender identities and expressions, however, sexual orientation-related criminalizing provisions may apply to transgender persons as well.

India   Bangladesh

Indonesia

This map was produced by the cartography unit of the Asian Development Bank. The boundaries, colors, denominations, and any other information shown on this map do not imply, on the part of the Asian Development Bank, any judgment on the legal status of any territory, or any other endorsement or acceptance of such boundaries, colors, denominations, or information.

B. ADB Study (2024)

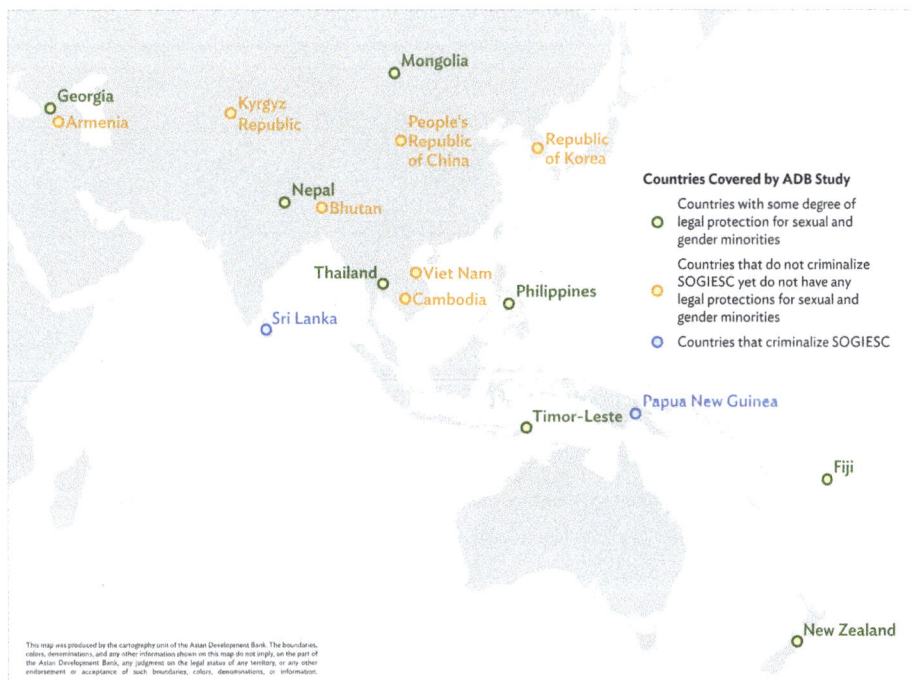

Mongolia

Georgia

Armenia

Kyrgyz Republic

People's Republic of China

Republic of Korea

Nepal

Bhutan

Countries Covered by ADB Study

○ (green) Countries with some degree of legal protection for sexual and gender minorities

○ (yellow) Countries that do not criminalize SOGIESC yet do not have any legal protections for sexual and gender minorities

○ (blue) Countries that criminalize SOGIESC

Thailand   Viet Nam

Cambodia   Philippines

Sri Lanka

Papua New Guinea

Timor-Leste

Fiji

New Zealand

This map was produced by the cartography unit of the Asian Development Bank. The boundaries, colors, denominations, and any other information shown on this map do not imply, on the part of the Asian Development Bank, any judgment on the legal status of any territory, or any other endorsement or acceptance of such boundaries, colors, denominations, or information.

ADB = Asian Development Bank; SGM = sexual and gender minorities; SOGIESC = sexual orientation, gender identity and expression, and sex characteristics.

Source: ADB; J.Arzinos, C. Medina Soto, and C. Cortez. 2021. *Equality of Opportunity for Sexual and Gender Minorities.* Washington, DC: World Bank.

The following is a list of 11 legal and policy actions for consideration to address the gaps in existing legal frameworks and to foster the inclusion of sexual and gender minorities. (A more comprehensive set of recommendations on legal and regulatory reforms can be found at the end of the discussion on each indicator set in this report.)

(i)   **Repeal anti-SOGIESC criminal laws.** Repeal laws that criminalize behaviors and activities related to SOGIESC.

(ii)   **Enhance educational inclusivity and combat discrimination.** Introduce comprehensive legal protections and conduct training and awareness campaigns to combat discrimination and SOGIESC-based bullying and harassment in educational settings. Enact regulatory reforms to foster more inclusive educational systems for both students and teachers who identify as sexual and gender minority members.

(iii)   **Strengthen workplace protections and inclusive policies.** Amend existing laws or enact new laws and regulations to explicitly prohibit discrimination based on SOGIESC at the workplace.

(iv)   **Ensure nondiscriminatory public service access.** Establish a comprehensive legal framework ensuring nondiscrimination in providing public services to LGBTI people.

(v)   **Ensure self-identified gender recognition.** Ensure legal gender recognition for trans and gender-diverse people based on self-identification.

(vi)   **Ensure bodily autonomy for intersex individuals.** Establish a comprehensive legal framework ensuring the bodily autonomy of intersex individuals, including intersex children.

(vii)   **Enable freedom of association for minority organizations.** Create an enabling environment for sexual and gender minority organizations to register and operate freely by introducing new laws or amending current laws/regulations.

(viii)   **Prohibit hate crimes against gender minorities.** Enact or amend laws specifically prohibiting hate crimes against sexual and gender minorities.

(ix)   **Implement hate crime data collection mechanisms.** Establish monitoring mechanisms to periodically collect data on hate crimes based on SOGIESC to understand the nature and extent of these violent acts.

(x)   **Conduct sensitization training for professionals.** Design and implement training programs for police, judicial officials, teachers, and health care professionals to sensitize them about SOGIESC and address biases and misconceptions.

(xi)   **Launch inclusive public awareness campaigns.** Implement public awareness campaigns aimed at dispelling myths and misconceptions about diverse SOGIESC. Create a supportive social environment for the inclusion of LGBTI people.

INTRODUCTION

I

1.   Sexual and gender minorities in Asia and the Pacific experience multiple and intersecting forms of discrimination, which adversely affect their lives as well as the economic and social development of their countries. Understanding these challenges is the first step toward creating development interventions to improve the lives of those involved. This study is among the first efforts by multilateral development agencies to examine the legal barriers to the effective and comprehensive development and inclusion of sexual and gender minorities. This study responds to the collective commitment to leave no one behind and promote inclusive development where people of diverse sexual orientation, gender identity and expression, and sex characteristics (SOGIESC) benefit equally.

2.   Systems and frameworks to measure the development outcomes and social and economic participation of sexual and gender minorities in the Asia and Pacific region are still in their infancy. Thus, data on the impact of stigma and discrimination on development outcomes at the population level are scarce. Yet, in all countries in the Asia and Pacific region, we can identify how stigma and discrimination reinforce legal barriers to full and effective inclusion. Documenting and analyzing the legal barriers to the inclusion of sexual and gender minorities through robust research is a key step in advancing inclusive development. This report, titled *Assessment of the Legal Status of Sexual and Gender Minorities in 17 Countries in Asia and the Pacific,* examines the legal discrimination against sexual and gender minorities by comparing the inclusion of these groups in laws and regulations with other population groups.

3.   The study found that sexual and gender minorities face systemic hurdles to access and effectively contribute to markets and services—such as education, labor markets, social protection, and public services—as a result of criminalization and a lack of antidiscrimination laws and regulations. Exclusion from these markets and services impedes their human development and economic opportunity. Further, sexual and gender minorities experience barriers and restrictions in expressing their identities, exercising freedom of association, forming relationship or marriages, and applying for legal gender recognition.

4.   The study also found that in many countries, hate crimes and hate speech against sexual and gender minorities are prevalent; in other countries, they experience persecution. Recent empirical evidence from North Macedonia and Serbia suggests that criminalization of sexual and gender minorities diminishes opportunities and spaces for them to participate in and contribute to economic growth, often at the expense of the country's overall development.[1]

---

[1]   A. Flores et al. 2023. *The Economic Cost of Exclusion Based on Sexual Orientation, Gender Identity and Expression, and Sex Characteristics in the Labor Market in the Republic of Serbia.* Washington, DC: World Bank; A. Flores et al. 2023. *The Economic Cost of Exclusion Based on Sexual Orientation, Gender Identity and Expression, and Sex Characteristics in the Labor Market in the Republic of North Macedonia.* Washington, DC: World Bank; M.V. Lee Badgett. 2014. *The Economic Cost of Stigma and the Exclusion of LGBT People: A Case Study of India (English).* Washington, DC: World Bank.

5.   The report builds on the methodology of the World Bank's *Equality of Opportunity for Sexual and Gender Minorities* (EQOSOGI) study published in 2021.[2] The EQOSOGI project gathered and analyzed multicountry data on laws and regulations that enable or hinder social and economic inclusion of sexual and gender minorities and their access to social, economic, civil, and political domains and development activities in a country through six indicator sets (para. 7). EQOSOGI's indicator sets and methodology offer countries and development institutes a framework to measure whether the countries provide an enabling environment for sexual and gender minorities' access to markets and services. The EQOSOGI data were collected in 2020 in 16 pilot countries covering a range of World Bank regions and income groups: Bangladesh, Canada, Costa Rica, India, Indonesia, Jamaica, Japan, Kosovo, Lebanon, Mexico, Mozambique, Nigeria, South Africa, Tunisia, Ukraine, and Uruguay.

6.   This Asian Development Bank (ADB) study uses the same six indicator sets to assess and analyze the legal and regulatory frameworks that directly or indirectly criminalize or discriminate against sexual and gender minorities. Data collected for the ADB study will also contribute to the publication of a joint ADB and World Bank second edition of the EQOSOGI report, which aims to cover 64 countries across the globe.

---

[2]   J. Arzinos, C. Medina Soto, and C. Cortez. 2021. *Equality of Opportunity for Sexual and Gender Minorities*. Washington, DC: World Bank.

A. Indicator Sets

7.   This report builds on six indicator sets developed by the World Bank for the EQOSOGI research initiative (footnote 2). These cover laws and regulations that affect sexual and gender minorities' access to markets and social, economic, civil, and political spaces in a country. These laws influence the ability of sexual and gender minorities to effectively contribute to and benefit from a country's economic development. Fundamental to this question is whether a country considers sexual and gender minorities to be "legal"—that is, whether the legal system permits any degree of inclusion of sexual and gender minorities. This question is complemented through six indicator sets to assess sexual and gender minorities' access to other social and economic domains. Each indicator consists of various data points to assess a range of legal protections:

(i)   **Decriminalization of sexual and gender minorities.** This indicator set examines the level of decriminalization or criminalization of SOGIESC-related behavior, including consensual same-sex activities and gender expression. It also monitors whether sexual and gender minorities are indirectly targeted by vagrancy, public nuisance, or morality-related laws.

(ii)   **Access to education.** This indicator set assesses the presence of laws promoting equal access to public education for sexual and gender minorities. It also examines laws and policies aimed at preventing discrimination and bullying of these students.

(iii)   **Access to labor markets.** This indicator set identifies antidiscrimination laws and regulations to protect sexual and gender minorities from discrimination in various areas of employment relations—including recruitment, wages, remuneration, unfair dismissal, and pension benefits—in both public and private sector workplaces.

(iv)   **Access to public services and social protection.** This indicator set measures laws and regulations that enable sexual and gender minorities to equally access health care and social protection, including housing, unemployment benefits, old age benefits, etc. It also assesses the presence of legal frameworks that enable legal gender recognition for trans and gender-diverse persons on a self-identification basis.

(v)   **Civil and political inclusion.** This indicator set examines the level of political participation by sexual and gender minorities and the ability of lesbian, gay, bisexual, transgender, and intersex (LGBTI) civil society organizations (CSOs) to operate without fear of persecution. It also assesses laws that enable sexual and gender minorities to form civil unions or marriages, adopt children, and access assisted reproductive technologies available to heterosexual couples.

(vi) **Protection from hate crimes.** Finally, this indicator set assesses whether existing laws and regulations provide protection from hate crimes against sexual and gender minorities. It also assesses the laws mandating the establishment of mechanisms to collect data, monitor the extent of hate crimes, and provide support services to victims of SOGIESC-based hate crimes.

B. Data Collection and Selection of Countries

8. ADB recruited a team of consultants to collect and analyze laws and regulations for the study. They used the standardized questionnaire of the World Bank's EQOSOGI initiative (Appendix) to assess existing laws and regulations under each of the six indicators (para. 7). The study used three sources to gather relevant data: (i) contributions from lawyers, ombudsperson institutions, judges, academics, and CSOs collected through the standardized questionnaire; (ii) public records and government databases, as well as relevant data from international legal databases and human rights organizations, such as the International Lesbian, Gay, Bisexual, Trans and Intersex Association (ILGA) World and Equal Index; and (iii) additional desk research of literature beyond laws and regulations, e.g., technical reports produced by United Nations agencies and CSOs.

9. The team spent 12 months (January 2022–2023) identifying and consulting legal experts, academics, civil society representatives, and government officials to ensure the quality of data collection. A minimum threshold of 10 fully completed questionnaires was set for all sample countries, and more than 170 experts contributed to the data collection by responding to the standardized questionnaire. The team received overall guidance from the World Bank's resource persons throughout the data collection process. ADB's country resource persons and legal consultants analyzed and cross-checked the data collected through the questionnaires with their desk research to ensure accuracy. When the team identified any discrepancies, follow-up was carried out with the expert contributors through email and phone calls to conduct additional research and seek clarifications. The legal consultants for each country prepared individual coding sheets with the legal and regulatory assessment; these were reviewed by ADB's team lead for the research initiative and World Bank resource persons for quality assurance. Further, the study was reviewed by a panel of three external expert reviewers. It was also reviewed by a panel of regional LGBTI CSOs and ADB's interdepartmental technical experts.

10. Seventeen countries were selected to represent several key characteristics (Table 1): (i) diversity of geographies (representing all ADB subregions and two non-developing member countries); (ii) developing member countries (DMCs) where ADB is currently implementing its operations; (iii) various legal traditions of the world; and (iv) a population of more than 750,000. The ADB sample excluded countries already included in the World Bank EQOSOGI pilot (Bangladesh, India, and Indonesia).

11. Data presented in this report, *Assessment of the Legal Status of Sexual and Gender Minorities in 17 Countries in Asia and the Pacific,* reflect laws and regulations enforced on or before 1 January 2023.

Table 1: Countries Covered by ADB's Study

Region	Country
Central and West Asia	Armenia, Georgia, Kyrgyz Republic
Southeast Asia	Cambodia, Philippines, Thailand, Timor-Leste, Viet Nam
East Asia	People's Republic of China, Mongolia
South Asia	Bhutan, Nepal, Sri Lanka
Pacific	Fiji, Papua New Guinea
Non-DMC	Republic of Korea, New Zealand

ADB = Asian Development Bank, DMC = developing member country.
Source: ADB.

C. Limitations

12.   The methodology used in this report has a few limitations. First, this report is not a comprehensive analysis of the laws and regulations on issues that affect sexual and gender minorities. For example, the study does not examine laws and regulations that govern informal labor markets. Further, the current indicator sets do not include access to financial resources and services, such as microfinance and commercial finance programs. Additionally, it does not consider customary laws and military penal laws. Second, the report does not examine the factors contributing to the existence or lack of specific laws or non-implementation of existing positive laws and regulations. Third, the report does not assess the private sector's practices beyond the labor laws and regulations that govern private labor markets. Fourth, the report does not assess laws and regulations that provide protections to lesbian and bisexual women against gender-based discrimination and violence. Finally, the report does not include data about the impacts of the enforcement or nonenforcement of laws and policies. Future iterations of the report will attempt to address these limitations through revised and expanded indicator sets.

III SETTING THE CONTEXT: A CASE FOR SOGIESC INCLUSION

13.   The ability to decide how we express our sexuality and gender identity is fundamental to human dignity. Being unable to live according to who one is constitutes a deprivation that goes to the heart of human development and freedom.

14.   The criminalization of SOGIESC creates structural barriers for LGBTI people in relation to exercising basic freedoms and rights and, consequently, pushes them to the margins of society. It also fuels stigma and, consequently, violence and abuse of LGBTI people. Empirical studies from across the world illustrate that decriminalization of SOGIESC results in reduced rates of assaults and violence against LGBTI people.[3] At the macro level, discrimination, stigma, and exclusion of sexual and gender minorities can have a significant economic impact (Box 1). Further, discrimination affects the central drivers of human development—health, education, and access to labor markets. For example, recent data suggest a strong correlation between decriminalization of same-sex activities and improved health outcomes. A study conducted by the United Nations Development Programme (UNDP), O'Neill Institute for National and Global Health, Georgetown University, and the Global Network of People Living with HIV (GNP+) suggests that HIV rates are significantly higher in population groups in countries where same-sex activities are criminalized, and criminalization is actively enforced. The importance of the capability to exist as an LGBTI person is reflected in the first indicator set, which focuses on the **Decriminalization of Sexual and Gender Minorities**.

15.   Prevalent stigma and prejudice against LGBTI people result in their structural and systemic exclusion from various domains of society, including access to education, labor markets, public services, social protection programs, and civil and political spaces. Lack of institutionalized protections for LGBTI people can create conditions for discrimination and exclusion in educational institutions, employment, public services, and civil and political domains. Research from several countries in Asia and the Pacific shows that LGBTI students in Asia are subjected to bullying and discrimination, resulting in higher rates of dropout and absenteeism and lower rates of educational attainment.[4] Studies across the Asia and Pacific region show how prevalent prejudices, low education rates, and inadequate vocational training exclude sexual and gender minorities from workplace opportunities.[5] Research from Asia has identified exclusion during hiring, job retention, and promotion, with transgender people particularly at risk of exclusion in country contexts where legal gender recognition is lacking (footnote 5).

---

[3]   Amnesty International. 2008. *Love, Hate, and the Law: Decriminalizing Homosexuality*. London: Amnesty International.

[4]   UNESCO. 2015. *From Insult to Inclusion: Asia-Pacific Report on School Bullying, Violence and Discrimination on the Basis of Sexual Orientation and Gender Identity*. Bangkok: UNESCO.

[5]   UNDP and ILO. 2018. *LGBTI People and Employment: Discrimination Based on Sexual Orientation, Gender Identity and Expression, and Sex Characteristics in China, the Philippines and Thailand*. Bangkok: UNDP; S. Winter et al. 2018. *Denied Work: An Audit of Employment Discrimination on the Basis of Gender Identity in South-East Asia*. Bangkok: APTN and UNDP.

Box 1: Cost of Stigma and Discrimination on Individual Businesses and the Economy

Stigma and discrimination have a cumulative impact on both individual businesses and the national economy. A 2014 United States Agency for International Development (USAID) study of low- and middle-income economies showed that each additional right for lesbian, gay, bisexual, and transgender people, measured according to the Global Index on Legal Recognition of Homosexual Orientation and the Transgender Rights Index, is associated with an increase of $320 in per capita gross domestic product (GDP), totaling up to 3% of GDP. A 2014 study in India found that excluding sexual and gender minorities, by means of stigma and exclusion based on sexual orientation, gender identity and expression, and sex characteristics (SOGIESC), led to weaker economic development. The study contended that SOGIESC-based exclusion lowered productivity and output through employment discrimination, labor supply constraints, and increased social and health service expenses, diverting resources from potentially more effective uses. The costs of lesbian, gay, bisexual, transgender, and intersex exclusion, according to this study, could be up to 1.7% of GDP, the equivalent of $32 billion. Researchers have taken various approaches to understanding the relationship between discrimination and individual businesses. Business leaders have noted that stigma and discrimination in the workplace can result in lost productivity. Limitations are placed on the ability to hire and retain workers, maintain high levels of workplace satisfaction and low levels of conflict, and attract a wider customer base. Research shows that greater inclusion of sexual and gender minorities is associated with higher stock prices, profitability, and productivity.

Sources: M. V. Lee Badgett et al. 2014. *The Relationship between LGBT Inclusion and Economic Development: Emerging Economies*. USAID and Williams Institute; M. V. Lee Badgett, K. Waaldijk, and Y. van der Meulen Rodgers. 2019. *The Relationship between LGBT Inclusion and Economic Development: Macro-Level Evidence. World Development* 120: pp. 1–14.

16.   Discrimination against people with diverse SOGIESC results in underinvestment in human capital development and, in turn, lost opportunities for economic inclusion and growth. Empirical research from Asia has also established a causal relationship between the experience of anti-LGBTI discrimination and increased health problems among sexual and gender minorities.[6] Poor health can limit a worker's productivity and increase the health care burden on the national economy. Besides decriminalization, there is a need to institutionalize safeguards against SOGIESC-based discrimination in these sectors. Detailed measures fostering inclusion of sexual and gender minorities are outlined in indicator sets focusing on **Access to Education, Access to Labor Markets, and Access to Public Services and Social Protection**.

17.   Transforming societal attitudes toward LGBTI people necessitates both social change and legal reforms, often spearheaded by the LGBTI community itself. Yet, barriers persist in civil and political participation as a result of various structural challenges, such as fear of reprisals, absence of legal gender recognition, and inadequate support for SOGIESC groups in exercising freedom of association. These challenges are detailed under the **Civil and Political Inclusion** indicator set.

---

[6]   R. Testa et al. 2015. *Development of the Gender Minority Stress and Resilience Measure. Psychology of Sexual Orientation and Gender Diversity* 2(1): 65–77; T.T.M Duc et al. 2020. *Sexual Self-Disclosure, Internalized Homophobia and Depression Symptoms among Sexual Minority Women in Vietnam. Health Psychology Open* 7(2): July–December; K.K.H. Tan and A.T. Saw. 2022. *Prevalence and Correlates of Mental Health Difficulties amongst LGBTQ People in Southeast Asia: A Systematic Review. Journal of Gay & Lesbian Mental Health* 27(4).

18.   Stigma and prejudice also create conditions for SOGIESC-based hate crimes. These hate crimes inflict physical and emotional harm, create fear and isolation within communities, and perpetuate a cycle of vulnerability, hindering their sense of safety, well-being, and inclusion in society (footnote 3). Hate crimes and violence can also prevent LGBTI people from fully participating in economic activities and society in general. The importance of these dimensions of development is reflected under the indicator set addressing **Protection from Hate Crimes**.

19.   Against the backdrop described here, with the limitations in health, education, and work experience, LGBTI people are often unable to live up to their full potential as workers, leaders, and consumers.[7]

---

[7]   M. V. Lee Badgett. 2014. *The Relationship between LGBT Inclusion and Economic Development: An Analysis of Emerging Economies*. USAID and Williams Institute; M. V. Lee Badgett, K. Waaldijk, and Y. van der Meulen Rodgers. 2019. The Relationship between LGBT Inclusion and Economic Development: Macro-Level Evidence. *World Development* 120: pp. 1–14.

THE STATE OF LEGAL INCLUSION OF SEXUAL AND GENDER MINORITIES IN ASIA AND THE PACIFIC

IV

A. Decriminalization of Sexual and Gender Minorities

20. The criminalization of sexual and gender minorities violates their right to live freely from discrimination and puts them at greater risk of violence and abuse. Criminalizing sexual and gender minorities also adversely affects the overall well-being and health outcomes of individuals and communities and poses barriers to providing effective health care services to a country's population. For example, criminalizing sexual orientation and gender identity is more likely to socially exclude LGBTI people, discourage their meaningful interaction with health services, and threaten healthy behaviors and decision-making.[8] There is compelling evidence that links the criminalization of same-sex activities with the heightened HIV risk of men who have sex with men (MSM). According to findings shared by an HIV Policy Lab study, in 2019, MSM were at 26 times higher risk of getting infected with HIV than the rest of the adult male population.[9] Additionally, MSM who live in countries where SOGIESC-related behavior is criminalized are two times more likely to be living with HIV than those living in countries without such criminalization (footnote 9). This indicator looks at:

(i) Criminalization of SOGIESC

(ii) Provisions that restrict gender expression (laws on "cross-dressing")

(iii) Indirect criminalization through vagrancy, nuisance, or public morality laws

(iv) Legal age of consent for same-sex activities

(v) Provisions that criminalize certain conduct of people living with HIV

(vi) Provisions for the incarceration of transgender prisoners according to their gender identity

1. Findings

21. Figure 1 presents the key findings for this indicator set.

---

8 Amnesty International. 2018. *Body Politics: A Primer on Criminalization of Sexuality and Reproduction*. London: Amnesty International.

9 M. Kavanagh et al. 2021. Law, Criminalisation and HIV in the World: Have Countries that Criminalise Achieved More or Less Successful Pandemic Response? *BMJ Global Health* 6: e006315.

Figure 1: Decriminalization of Sexual and Gender Minorities

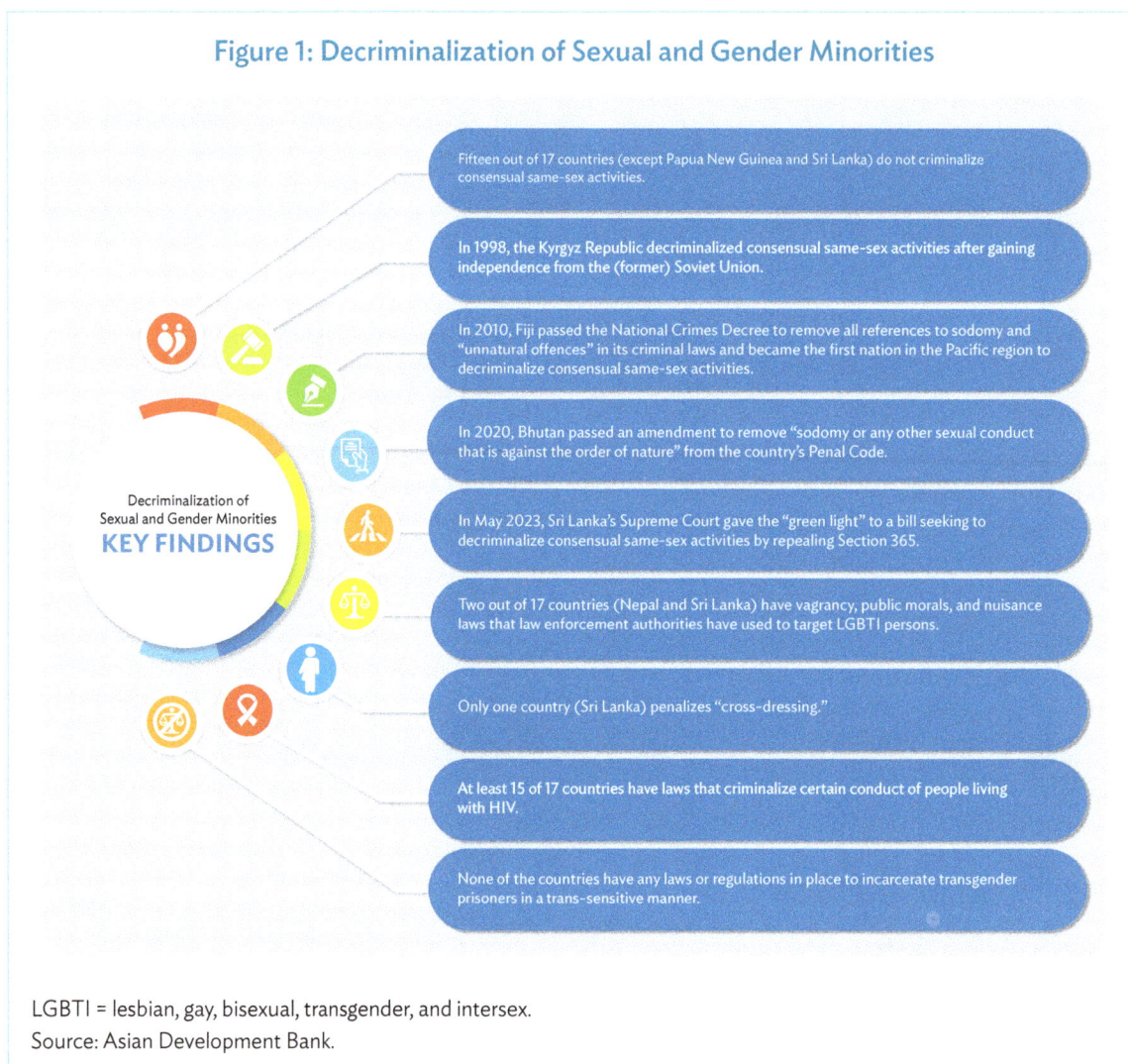

Decriminalization of
Sexual and Gender Minorities
KEY FINDINGS

Fifteen out of 17 countries (except Papua New Guinea and Sri Lanka) do not criminalize consensual same-sex activities.

In 1998, the Kyrgyz Republic decriminalized consensual same-sex activities after gaining independence from the (former) Soviet Union.

In 2010, Fiji passed the National Crimes Decree to remove all references to sodomy and "unnatural offences" in its criminal laws and became the first nation in the Pacific region to decriminalize consensual same-sex activities.

In 2020, Bhutan passed an amendment to remove "sodomy or any other sexual conduct that is against the order of nature" from the country's Penal Code.

In May 2023, Sri Lanka's Supreme Court gave the "green light" to a bill seeking to decriminalize consensual same-sex activities by repealing Section 365.

Two out of 17 countries (Nepal and Sri Lanka) have vagrancy, public morals, and nuisance laws that law enforcement authorities have used to target LGBTI persons.

Only one country (Sri Lanka) penalizes "cross-dressing."

At least 15 of 17 countries have laws that criminalize certain conduct of people living with HIV.

None of the countries have any laws or regulations in place to incarcerate transgender prisoners in a trans-sensitive manner.

LGBTI = lesbian, gay, bisexual, transgender, and intersex.
Source: Asian Development Bank.

a.   Criminalization of Homosexual Acts

22.   Except for Papua New Guinea (PNG) and Sri Lanka, all analyzed countries do not criminalize consensual same-sex activities. **PNG** explicitly prohibits consensual same-sex activities between males under Article 212 of the Criminal Code.[10] Further, Article 210 of PNG's Criminal Code criminalizes sexual relations that are against the "order of nature," including consensual sexual relations between two females.[11] **Sri Lanka** borrowed the criminalizing provisions for consensual same-sex activities from the British anti-sodomy laws (Box IV.1).

23.   Article 365 of Sri Lanka's Penal Code (1885), as amended by the Penal Code (Amendment) Act (Act No. 22) (1995), punishes "unnatural offenses" (defined as "carnal intercourse against the order of nature with any man, woman or animal") with imprisonment of up to 10 years.[12] Moreover, Article 365A

---

[10]   Criminal Code Act of Papua New Guinea, 1974, Art. 212.

[11]   Criminal Code Act of Papua New Guinea, 1974, Art. 210.

[12]   Penal Code of Sri Lanka, 1885, Art. 365.

of the Penal Code criminalizes "acts of gross indecency" with a penalty of up to 2 years in prison and/or a fine.[13] While the study does not examine military penal laws, it is worth noting that same-sex activities among members of the armed forces are criminalized under the Military Act, 2016 in the **Republic of Korea**.[14] However, a 2022 Supreme Court ruling overturned the decision of military authorities against two gay men who had engaged in sexual relations at their private residence while they were off duty. The Court ruled that the use of Article 92(6) of the Military Act, 2016 against the two men "jeopardizes their autonomy, equality, and dignity."[15]

24.   In recent years, several South Asian countries have taken significant steps to decriminalize SOGIESC. In 2020, Bhutan passed an amendment to remove "sodomy or any other sexual conduct that is against the order of nature" from the country's Penal Code. In May 2023, Sri Lanka's Supreme Court approved a bill seeking to repeal Section 365, thereby decriminalizing same-sex activities.

b. Provisions Restricting Gender Expression

25.   Section 399 of Sri Lanka's Penal Code criminalizes gender impersonation, prohibiting nonnormative gender expression and further marginalizing transgender persons in society.[16]

c. Indirect Criminalization through Vagrancy, Nuisance, and Public Morals Laws

26.   In countries like the **Kyrgyz Republic** and **Nepal**, where consensual same-sex activities between adults are not criminalized or where the criminalizing provisions are not invoked to prosecute same-sex activity, LGBTI people are indirectly targeted with vagrancy, nuisance, and public morals laws. Often a legacy of the colonial rulers, these laws give discretionary powers to law enforcement authorities to harass, intimidate, and arbitrarily arrest LGBTI persons and prevent LGBTI persons from living and participating in society freely and with dignity.[17] **Sri Lanka**'s Vagrancy Ordinance No. 4, 1841, has several broad provisions[18] that the police have used to harass and arrest lesbians and transgender persons.[19] In **Nepal**, Section 2 of Some Public (Crime and Punishment) Act 2027 (1970) contains vague provisions to prevent "obscene show, word, gesture" in public spaces[20] and has been reportedly used against transgender persons.[21]

d. Legal Age of Consent for Same-Sex Activities

27.   None of the countries analyzed distinguish the legal age for consensual sex for heterosexual and homosexual relations.

---

[13] Penal Code of Sri Lanka, 1885, Art. 365A.

[14] The Military Act of Republic of Korea, 2016, Art. 92(6).

[15] R. Thoreson. 2022. *South Korean Court Limits Military "Sodomy" Law: Greater Action Needed to Ensure Rights of LGBT People are Protected.* New York: Human Rights Watch.

[16] Penal Code of Sri Lanka, 1885.

[17] C. Roberts. 2022. *Vagrancy and Vagrancy-Type Laws in Colonial History and Today.* The Chinese University of Hong Kong.

[18] For instance, Sections 2 and 7(1)(b) of An Ordinance to Amend and Consolidate the Law Relating to Vagrants, 1841 (also known as Vagrancy Ordinance No. 4, last amended in 1947), Sri Lanka.

[19] International Court of Justice (ICJ). 2021. *Sri Lanka's Vagrants Ordinance No. 4 of 1841: A Colonial Relic Long Overdue for Repeal – A Briefing Paper.* Geneva: ICJ.

[20] Some Public (Crime and Punishment) Act of Nepal, 2027 (1970), Sect 2.

[21] UNDP and USAID. 2014. *Being LGBT in Asia: Nepal Country Profile.* Bangkok: UNDP.

e.   Criminalization of Certain Conduct of People Living with HIV

28.   Under this indicator, we analyzed laws concerning the sexual behavior of individuals with HIV. The emergence of HIV/AIDS in the region, initially linked with homosexuality, intensified societal prejudices and stigma against sexual and gender minorities. The disease was formerly termed the "gay plague," contributing to heightened fear and bias against gay men and transgender women. It also resulted in legal and regulatory reforms that criminalized the sexual relations of people living with HIV/ AIDS. Except for **Fiji, Mongolia,** and **Thailand**, all countries have enacted laws and regulations with broad criminalizing provisions for HIV/AIDS transmission. The criminalization of sexual conduct of people living with HIV/AIDS and the resulting stigma and prevalent biases against sexual and gender minorities prevent LGBTI people from outing themselves, which creates structural hurdles for them to access basic services such as health care.[22]

f.   Incarceration of Transgender and Gender-Diverse People

29.   Except for **New Zealand**, none of the studied countries imprison transgender and gender-diverse individuals based on their gender identity.[23] Additionally, these countries lack specific laws or regulations for transgender-sensitive incarceration. Research globally shows that this absence makes trans individuals, particularly trans women, highly susceptible to vulnerabilities, marginalization, violence, and sexual assault.[24] New Zealand implemented a Prison Operations Manual in 2016, establishing protocols for incarcerating trans and gender-diverse prisoners who have updated their birth certificate gender marker post-gender-affirming surgery.[25] However, these protocols have not been institutionalized through a legal or regulatory provision yet. In Thailand, the UNDP Country Office has collaborated with the Ministry of Justice to develop a manual for police authorities to manage their interactions with trans and gender-diverse people in a sensitive and dignified manner.[26]

2.   Recommendations

30.   Countries may consider adopting the following legal and policy practices to provide protections to sexual and gender minorities and to address existing legal gaps:

  (i)   Repeal laws and regulations that criminalize consensual same-sex activities between adults, including laws against sodomy.

  (ii)   Repeals laws and regulations that criminalize SOGIESC-related behavior, including laws on "cross-dressing."

---

[22] M. Kavanagh et al. 2021. Law, Criminalisation and HIV in the World: Have Countries that Criminalise Achieved More or Less Successful Pandemic Response? *BMJ Global Health* 6: e006315.

[23] Although no universal standard exists for trans-sensitive incarceration policies, several effective practices include consulting with trans prisoners about their placement preferences, offering gender-affirming care, and providing clothing aligned with their gender identity. For more details on good practices for management of trans prisoners, see UNDP. 2020. *Mapping of Good Practices for the Management of Transgender Prisoners*. Bangkok: UNDP.

[24] J. Rodgers, N. Asquith, and A. Dwyer. 2017. Cisnormativity, Criminalisation, Vulnerability: Transgender People in Prisons. *Issues Brief*. 12.

[25] Prison Operations Manual of New Zealand, 2016, M.03.05.

[26] UNDP Thailand. 2018. *UNDP Joins Forces with MOJ and Sisters Foundation to Improve Police Interactions with Transgender People*. Bangkok: UNDP.

(iii)   Repeal laws and regulations that explicitly or implicitly target LGBTI persons on vagrancy, public nuisance, and public morals grounds.

(iv)   Enact laws and regulations to protect LGBTI persons from police misconduct, including harassment, intimidation, arbitrary arrests, and other forms of violence.

(v)   Amend criminal laws and regulations to ensure that they only prohibit intentional transmission of HIV/AIDS where a person living with HIV knows his/her/their HIV status and acts with the intention to transmit it to another person.

(vi)   Enact laws and regulations to manage the housing of trans and gender-diverse prisoners in a trans-sensitive manner.

B. Access to Education

31.   Research on LGBTI exclusion and access to education in Asia and the Pacific reveals that prevalent social prejudices and stigmatization of diverse sexual orientations, gender identities and expressions, and sex characteristics result in social isolation and peer victimization of LGBTI students.[27] LGBTI students experience various forms of discrimination, including ostracization by fellow pupils and teachers, prohibition of gender expression through strict regulations around school uniforms, discrimination in school admission, and verbal and physical bullying and cyberbullying. Institutional discrimination, such as lack of representation of LGBTI persons in the textbooks and lack of gender-neutral toilets, is another prevalent form of exclusion of sexual and gender minorities.

32.   Studies in Asia have revealed that LGBTI students are subjected to discriminatory rules and bullying that lead to lower educational attainment, higher dropout rates, school absences, and youth suicide.[28] A review of data in Asia by the United Nations Educational, Scientific and Cultural Organization (UNESCO) notes, "There is evidence from the region that educational performance and achievement are also affected, leading to life-long impacts on employment and economic prospects and broader societal level impacts" (footnote 27).

33.   The Access to Education indicator set looks at laws and regulations (or lack thereof) that address various forms of discrimination experienced by LGBTI persons in educational settings. It assesses laws and regulations that provide for:

(i)   Prohibition of SOGIESC-based discrimination against students and/or teachers in educational settings (including in school admissions)

(ii)   Prohibition of SOGIESC-based bullying, cyberbullying, and harassment against students and/or teachers in educational settings

---

[27]   UNESCO. 2015. *From Insult to Inclusion: Asia-Pacific Report on School Bullying, Violence and Discrimination on the Basis of Sexual Orientation and Gender Identity*. Bangkok: UNESCO.

[28]   UNESCO. 2014. *Bullying Targeting Secondary School Students Who Are or Are Perceived to Be Transgender or Same-Sex Attracted: Types, Prevalence, Impact, Motivation and Preventive Measures in 5 Provinces of Thailand*. Bangkok: UNESCO, Mahidol University, and Plan International.

(iii)   Revision of textbooks to employ SOGIESC-inclusive language and mandatory training for teachers, including revision of sexuality education curricula to employ inclusive language

(iv)   Mechanisms for reporting complaints about SOGIESC-based discrimination in educational settings

(v)   Permission for students to dress according to their gender identity

1.   Findings

34.   Figure 2 presents the key findings of the study for this indicator set.

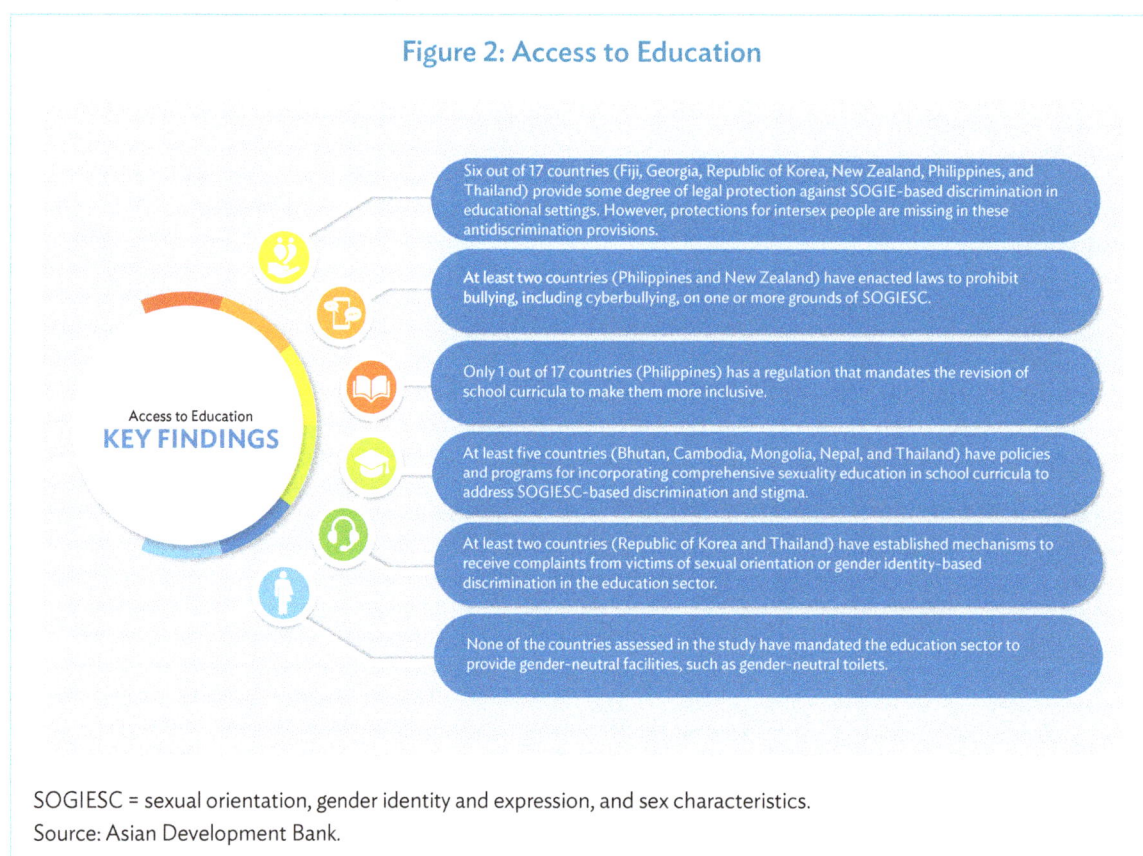

Figure 2: Access to Education

Access to Education
KEY FINDINGS

Six out of 17 countries (Fiji, Georgia, Republic of Korea, New Zealand, Philippines, and Thailand) provide some degree of legal protection against SOGIE-based discrimination in educational settings. However, protections for intersex people are missing in these antidiscrimination provisions.

At least two countries (Philippines and New Zealand) have enacted laws to prohibit bullying, including cyberbullying, on one or more grounds of SOGIESC.

Only 1 out of 17 countries (Philippines) has a regulation that mandates the revision of school curricula to make them more inclusive.

At least five countries (Bhutan, Cambodia, Mongolia, Nepal, and Thailand) have policies and programs for incorporating comprehensive sexuality education in school curricula to address SOGIESC-based discrimination and stigma.

At least two countries (Republic of Korea and Thailand) have established mechanisms to receive complaints from victims of sexual orientation or gender identity-based discrimination in the education sector.

None of the countries assessed in the study have mandated the education sector to provide gender-neutral facilities, such as gender-neutral toilets.

SOGIESC = sexual orientation, gender identity and expression, and sex characteristics.
Source: Asian Development Bank.

a.   Legal Protections for Students against SOGIESC-based Discrimination

35.   The majority of the analyzed countries do not have comprehensive legal protections against SOGIESC-based discrimination in schools and educational institutions. However, Georgia, Fiji, the Republic of Korea, Nepal, New Zealand, the Philippines, and Thailand provide some legal protections against discrimination based on an individual's SOGIESC (Table 2).

Table 2: Good Practices to Prohibit SOGIESC-Based Discrimination in Education Settings

Measure	Country	Example
Prohibition of discrimination based on SOGIESC in access to education	Georgia, Fiji, Nepal, New Zealand, Philippines, Republic of Korea, Thailand	Law on the Elimination of All Forms of Discrimination 2014 of Georgia establishes guarantees against all forms of discrimination based on SOGIESC and applies to education settings.[a]
Prohibition of discrimination on the basis of SOGIESC during the admission process	New Zealand	Section 57 of New Zealand's Human Rights Act 1993 provides extensive legal protections against various forms of discrimination based on sexual orientation in educational settings, including protections against refusal to admit or admitting them on "less favorable" terms and conditions and denial of services or benefits.[b]

SOGIESC = sexual orientation, gender identity and expression, and sex characteristics.
[a] Law of Georgia on Elimination of All Forms of Discrimination, 2014, Art. 1.
[b] Human Rights Act of New Zealand, 1993, Sec. 57.
Source: Compiled by authors.

b. Protections Against Bullying and Cyberbullying

36.   The **Philippines** has instituted explicit prohibitions against sexual orientation and gender identity-based bullying in school and education institutions under the Implementing Rules and Regulations of Republic Act No. 10627 of 2013 (entry into force in April 2019) and the Safe Spaces Act of 2019.[29] These laws offer comprehensive protection against various types of bullying, including cyberbullying. The Philippines has enacted policies to curb bullying in educational settings, such as the Commission on Higher Education Guidelines prohibiting acts like "misogynistic, transphobic, homophobic, and sexist slurs," as well as "unwanted sexual remarks and comments made online, publicly or through private messages."[30]

37.   **New Zealand** has enacted the Harmful Digital Communications Act, 2015, Section 6(1), which prohibits any form of digital communication that aims to "denigrate" an individual based on their sexual orientation.[31] The act also allows victims of sexual orientation-based bullying to bring a complaint to independent commissions for remedy.

c. Comprehensive Sexuality Education

38.   Except for the Philippines, none of the countries analyzed in the study have laws or regulations that mandate the revision of school curricula to make them inclusive of sexual and gender minorities, nor do they have any laws or regulations that require schools and educational institutions to incorporate sexuality education curricula to address harmful stereotypes and prejudices against sexual and gender minorities. The **Philippines** has adopted a regulation, DO No. 32, S. 2017—Gender-Responsive Basic Education Policy of 2017 (entry into force in June 2017), that regulates the Department of Education

---

[29] Implementing Rules and Regulations of Republic Act No. 10627, 2013 (entry into force in April 2019), Sec. 3(B)(1); Safe Spaces Act of Philippines, 2019, Sec. 11.

[30] Commission on Higher Education. 2022. Guidelines on Gender-Based Sexual Harassment in Higher Education Institutions.

[31] Harmful Digital Communications Act of New Zealand, 2015, Sec. 6(1).

to incorporate concepts of gender and sexuality in their totality and to institutionalize comprehensive sexuality education in school curricula for grades K–12.[32] Further, DO No. 31, S. 2018 calls for the implementation of comprehensive sexuality education that is gender-responsive and rights-based.[33] Positive policy and programmatic initiatives are in place across several countries in the region (Table 3).

Table 3: Examples of SOGIESC Inclusion in Sexuality Education Policies and Programs

Country	Example
Bhutan	**Bhutan** institutionalized the incorporation of sexuality education in schools in 2021 by adopting a National Strategic Framework on Comprehensive Sexuality Education that covers various topics, including adolescent sexual and reproductive health and issues of the LGBTI community.[a]
Cambodia	The Ministry of Education, Youth and Sport in **Cambodia** announced that comprehensive sexuality education would be incorporated into the school curricula for children aged 13 and above and this would include sexual and gender diversities to address bullying in schools.[b]
Mongolia	In 2018, **Mongolia** became one of the first countries in the region to incorporate the United Nations multi-agency International Technical Guidance on Comprehensive Sexuality Education, which addresses issues related to human sexuality and non-binary genders in a comprehensive manner.[c]
Nepal	Sexual orientation and gender identity issues have been included in the school curriculum for Classes 6, 7, and 8 in **Nepal** since 2014.[d]
Thailand	In 2019, **Thailand** issued revised health and physical education textbooks for Grades 1–12, which aim to include positive representation of sexual and gender minorities.[e] The revised curriculum aims to address SOGIESC-based discrimination and stigma based on sexual orientation, gender identity and expression and to promote social acceptance and respect for the human rights of lesbian, gay, bisexual, transgender, and intersex students in school settings.

LGBTI = lesbian, gay, bisexual, transgender, and intersex; SOGIESC = sexual orientation, gender identity and expression, and sex characteristics.

[a] N. Dorji. 2022. Training Teachers and School Counsellors on Comprehensive Sexuality Education. *Kuensel*. 4 January.
[b] M. Blomberg. 2019. Cambodia to Teach LGBT+ Issues in Schools to Tackle Discrimination. Openly. 10 December.
[c] M. Unurzul. 2020. Health Education Issues Discussed. *Mongolian National News Agency*. 21 October.
[d] UNDP and UNESCO. 2015. *Meeting Report: Asia Pacific Consultation on School Bullying Based on Sexual Orientation and Gender Identity/Expression*. Bangkok.
[e] UNESCO. 2019. Let's Talk about Sex: Thai-Language Sexuality Education Guidance. Launched 26 June. Bangkok: UNESCO.
Source: Compiled by authors.

39.   **Thailand's** Gender Equality Act established an inquiry committee, WorLorPor, to investigate complaints of gender-based discrimination and provide remedies to victims. The WorLorPor Committee has the authority of a judicial body, and its recommendations are binding. According to an assessment report prepared by UNDP and the Ministry of the Thai Department of Women's Affairs and Family Development, the WorLorPor Committee has received most complaints from victims of discrimination in educational settings. For example, most of the complaints were submitted by trans students who were not allowed to wear a uniform according to their gender identity.[34]

---

[32] DO No. 32, S. 2017. Gender-Responsive Basic Education Policy, 2017.

[33] DO No. 31, S. 2018. Comprehensive Sexuality Education: Developing Responsible Youth vs. Rising Risks.

[34] UNDP and Department of Women's Affairs and Family Development of Ministry of Social Development and Human Security. 2020. *Assessment Report: Implementation of the Gender Equality Act B.E. 2558*. Bangkok.

31.   Further, the National Human Rights Commission of the **Republic of Korea** accepts complaints of SOGIESC-based discrimination in educational settings, among other sectors, and seeks to provide a remedy to the complainant.[35] However, its recommendations are not legally binding and thus cannot be enforced.

d.   Permission to Dress According to Gender Identity

40.   None of the analyzed countries have laws or regulations to ensure that schools have gender-neutral facilities, such as toilets and sports facilities. Regulations and policies around school uniforms are not considerate of transgender students' gender identities and expressions.

2.   Recommendations

41.   Countries may consider adopting the following legal and policy practices to address SOGIESC-based discrimination and foster the inclusion of sexual and gender minorities in the education sector:

(i)   Enact new laws and regulations or amend existing legal and regulatory instruments to provide explicit and comprehensive protection against SOGIESC-based discrimination in educational settings. Ensure existing anti-discriminatory laws and regulations for the education sector are harmonized and consistently used for sexual and gender minorities as well.

(ii)   Enact laws and regulations that address SOGIESC-based bullying and cyberbullying in educational settings and institutionalize monitoring, reporting, and support mechanisms for the victims.

(iii)   Enact laws and regulations that require the incorporation of comprehensive sexuality education to address SOGIESC-related stigma and myths.

(iv)   Enact laws and regulations that mandate teacher training to ensure SOGIESC-inclusive practices in pedagogy and classroom settings.

(v)   Enact laws and regulations to establish trans-sensitive infrastructure and practices (including gender-neutral facilities and uniforms) in educational settings.

C. Access to Labor Markets

43.   Nondiscrimination at the workplace and access to decent work is a fundamental right. However, this remains a context where LGBTI persons experience multifaceted discrimination. In one survey supported by UNDP, almost half of all respondents in the Philippines and Thailand had seen job advertisements that implicitly excluded LGBTI people from applying (footnote 5). Many surveys of LGBTI people indicate they have experienced discrimination and harassment in the workplace.[36]

---

[35] National Human Rights Commission Act of Korea, 2009, Arts 1, 2(4), and 3.

[36] UNDP and Williams Institute. 2014. *Surveying Nepal's Sexual and Gender Minorities: An Inclusive Approach.* Bangkok; UNDP. 2019. *Tolerance but Not Inclusion: A National Survey on Experiences of Discrimination and Social Attitudes towards LGBT People in Thailand.* Bangkok; World Bank. 2018. *Economic Inclusion of LGBTI Groups in Thailand.* Washington, DC: World Bank; M. V. Lee Badgett, A. Hasenbush, and W.E. Luhur. 2017. *LGBT Exclusion in Indonesia and Its Economic Effects.* Los Angeles, CA: The Williams Institute UCLA School of Law.

Experimental studies have been conducted to monitor and document discrimination experienced by transgender people in Malaysia, Singapore, Thailand, and Viet Nam. A study by UNDP, Curtin University, and the Asia Pacific Transgender Network (APTN) found that transgender people experienced discrimination and unfair treatment during recruitment and employment as a result of their gender identity.[37] The study also found that transgender job applicants received fewer positive responses from potential employers than cisgender (non-transgender) applicants (Box 2). Similarly, a study by the International Labour Organization (ILO) and UNDP found that there were limited protections for LGBTI people in the labor markets in the People's Republic of China, Thailand, and the Philippines, and that they experience discriminatory treatment in the workplace yet have little to no recourse to remedy unfair treatment (footnote 5).

Box 2: Discrimination against Transgender People in the Employment Sector in Southeast Asia

A 2019 study conducted by Curtin University, United Nations Development Programme (UNDP) Asia Pacific, and Asia Pacific Transgender Network (APTN) revealed severe discrimination against transgender persons in the employment sector in Malaysia, Singapore, Thailand, and Viet Nam. Transgender persons faced far greater difficulty in getting invited for an interview or even a positive response for their job applications in all job sectors compared with cisgender applicants with equivalent resumes.

Source: S. Winter et al. 2018. *Denied Work: An Audit of Employment Discrimination on the Basis of Gender Identity in South-East Asia.* Bangkok: APTN and UNDP.

---

44.   Several systemic and structural barriers prevent LGBTI persons from having access to equal opportunity for decent work, resulting in marginalization and perpetual cycles of poverty among this demographic group. The Access to Labor Markets indicator set looks at:

   (i)   Prohibition of SOGIESC-based workplace discrimination in public and private sectors (including in the recruitment process), including guaranteeing equal remuneration for work of equal value and prohibition of unfair dismissal based on their SOGIESC

   (ii)   Mechanisms for reporting complaints about SOGIESC-based discrimination

   (iii) Equal pension benefits to same-sex couples

   (iv)   Permission for employees to dress according to their gender identity and availability of inclusive facilities, for example gender-neutral toilets

1.   Findings

45.   Figure 3 presents the key findings of the study for this indicator.

---

[37]   S. Winter et al. 2018. *Denied Work: An Audit of Employment Discrimination on the Basis of Gender Identity in South-East Asia.* Bangkok: APTN and UNDP.

Figure 3: Access to Labor Markets

Access to Labor Market
KEY FINDINGS

Eight out of 17 countries (Fiji, Georgia, Republic of Korea, Mongolia, Nepal, New Zealand, Philippines, and Thailand) have some degree of legal or constitutional protection against SOGIE-based discrimination in the labor market. However, protections for intersex people are missing in these antidiscrimination provisions.

Five out of 17 countries (Fiji, Republic of Korea, Mongolia, New Zealand, and Philippines) provide explicit legal protections against SOGIESC-based discrimination during the recruitment process and against unfair dismissal based on an employee's SOGIESC.

Five out of 17 countries (Fiji, Republic of Korea, Mongolia, New Zealand, and Philippines) provide explicit legal protections for equal remuneration for equal work regardless of one's SOGIESC.

Only New Zealand legally recognizes same-sex partnerships and extends employment benefits to same-sex spouse.

At least 6 out of 17 countries (Fiji, Republic of Korea, Mongolia, New Zealand, Philippines, and Thailand) have institutionalized equality bodies or national human rights institutions to investigate complaints of discrimination based on sexual orientation and/or gender identity and expression.

None of the countries have enacted laws or regulations that mandate the provision of gender-neutral facilities, such as gender-neutral toilets.

SOGIESC = sexual orientation, gender identity and expression, and sex characteristics.
Source: Asian Development Bank.

a. Legal Protections against SOGIESC-Based Discrimination in the Labor Market

46. At least half of the analyzed countries provide some legal protections against SOGIESC-based discrimination in the labor market. Fiji, Georgia, Mongolia, New Zealand, and the Philippines have included a range of protections against discrimination based on sexual orientation and/or gender identity and expressions in their labor laws (Table 4).

47. In the **People's Republic of China,** while the legislative framework is silent on SOGIESC-based discrimination at the workplace, significant positive litigations have set legal precedence for the effective inclusion of transgender persons and antidiscrimination advocacy. For example, in 2020, a Beijing intermediate court ruled in favor of a transgender employee of an e-commerce firm, Dang Dang, in an illegal termination suit. The court ruled that the firm's refusal to approve sick leave for its employee's gender-reaffirming surgery was a violation of labor protections guaranteed by the country's laws.[38] The court ruling also embraced a more comprehensive concept of gender identity and expression:

> "The trend of modern society is towards increasingly rich diversity... We are accustomed to understanding society through our conception of biological sex, but there are some people who express their gender identity in accordance with their own life experiences. This kind of social expression—the existence of which is sustained—often requires us to renew our understanding and how we look at things" (footnote 38).

---

[38] D. Longarino. 2020. Was the Dang Dang Case a Successful Transgender Discrimination Lawsuit? *China Law Translate.* 15 September.

Table 4: Examples of Labor Laws That Prohibit Discrimination against Sexual and Gender Minorities

Country	Measure
Fiji	Fiji's Employment Relations Act 2007, which applies to both public and private sectors, provides explicit protections against discrimination based on a person's sexual orientation and gender identity and expression (the latter was added to the act during the 2015 Amendment). Measures include: • Prohibition of recruitment with less favorable pay and benefits • Prohibition of discriminatory access to training and promotion opportunities, unfair dismissal, and early retirement or forced resignations • Prohibition of medical examination, including HIV/AIDS screening, "in the course of a worker's employment"[a]
Georgia	A 2019 amendment of the Labor Code 2010 provides protections against all forms of discrimination in labor and precontractual relations, including when publishing a vacancy announcement and at the selection stage, on several grounds, including race, skin color, language, ethnic and social origin, nationality, origin, property or estate status, place of residence, age, gender, sexual orientation, disability, membership in religious, public, political, or other associations, including trade unions, marital status, political or other views, or other ground.[b]
Mongolia	The Revised Labor Code 2021 provides extensive legal protections to sexual and gender minorities in the labor sector, including discrimination in employment relations. It also mandates equal remuneration for employees performing work of equal value and prohibits unfair dismissal of an employee based on their sexual orientation and/or gender identity and expression.[c]
New Zealand	The Employment Relations Act 2000 includes sexual orientation in the prohibited grounds for discrimination.[d] Further, the Act reinforces the protections against discriminatory practices in the labor market outlined in the Human Rights Act 1993, such as discrimination in recruitment, in employment conditions at the workplace, and in opportunities for training and promotion; unfair dismissal; and forced resignation.[e]
Philippines	In the Philippines, the Magna Carta of Women, or Republic Act 9710, of 2009 includes sexual orientation among the prohibited grounds for discrimination. Further, the Magna Carta of Public Social Workers 2007 protects public social workers from discrimination on the basis of their sexual orientation, among other grounds.[f]

[a] Employment Relations Act of Fiji, 2007, Arts 6.2, 38.2, 75, 77.
[b] Labor Code of Georgia, 2019, Arts 2(3), 47.
[c] Labor Code of Mongolia, 2021, Arts 6.1, 6.2, 6.6, 80.
[d] Employment Relations Act of New Zealand, 2000, Sec. 105.
[e] Human Rights Act of New Zealand, 1993, Secs 21 and 22.
[f] Act Providing for the Magna Carta of Women, 2009, Sec.3; Magna Carta of Public Social Workers, 2007, Sec. 17.
Source: Compiled by authors.

48.   Similarly, in the **Philippines**, several government agencies have issued policy orders to prohibit discrimination on one or more grounds of SOGIESC. For example, Civil Service Commission Memorandum Circular No. 29-2010 protects against discrimination based on one or more grounds of sexual orientation, and gender identity and expression during the application process for civil service examinations. Recently, the Department of Social Welfare and Development called for respecting the right of transgender persons to wear a uniform that aligns with their gender identity.[39]

---

[39] Government of the Philippines, Department of Social Welfare and Development. 2016. *DSWD Promotes a Gender-Inclusive Workplace*. 29 September.

b. Mechanisms for Reporting Complaints about SOGIESC-Based Discrimination

49.   Fiji, the Republic of Korea, Mongolia, New Zealand, the Philippines, and Thailand have institutionalized equality bodies or national human rights institutions to investigate complaints of discrimination based on sexual orientation and/or gender identity and expression.

50.   In the **Philippines**, the Commission on Human Rights, established under the Magna Carta of Women (RA 9710), is mandated to investigate complaints from women and persons with diverse SOGIESC about discrimination committed by an individual or entity.[40] In **Mongolia**'s Labor Code 2021, the law empowers the victims of sexual orientation and/or gender identity-based discrimination to register a complaint with the National Human Rights Commission and relevant courts. The law also requires all employers to share with their employees the names and contact details of all government bodies and other entities that can receive and investigate such complaints.[41] **Thailand's** Gender Equality Act mandates the WorLorPor Committee to investigate complaints from victims of unfair dismissal and provide necessary remedies. The WorLorPor Committee has acted upon numerous complaints to provide necessary redress (Box 3).

Box 3: Implementation of the Gender Equality Act B.E. 2558 (2015) in Thailand

The Gender Equality Act B.E. 2558 (2015) marks an important milestone in that it is Thailand's first major antidiscrimination law that explicitly includes gender expression as a prohibited ground.[a] Specifically, the act prohibits any "unfair gender discrimination" on the basis that a person is male or female or has a "gender expression different from birth sex" (Sec. 3, para. 1). The application of the Gender Equality Act to lesbians, gays, and bisexuals remains unclear. Further, under the act, two separate equality bodies are created. The first committee is called the Gender Equality Promotion Committee (SorTorPor). Chaired by the prime minister, the committee is mandated to create policies and measures to promote gender equality in the public and private spheres in the central, regional, and local areas of Thailand. The second equality body is known as the Committee on Consideration of Unfair Gender Discrimination (WorLorPor Committee). It is mandated to receive cases of unfair gender discrimination, establish temporary measures to protect victims of gender discrimination, issue directives based on a case's decision, and submit complaints to the ombudsperson on behalf of the victims. According to a 2020 report prepared by the United Nations Development Programme (UNDP) and the Department of Women's Affairs and Family, the WorLorPor Committee adjudicated at least six complaints from transgender persons in 2019 and found the accused parties guilty of discrimination.

[a] Thailand Gender Equality Act B.E. 2558 (2015), Sec. 3(1).

Source: UNDP and Department of Women's Affairs and Family Development of the Ministry of Social Development and Human Security. 2020. *Assessment Report: Implementation of the Gender Equality Act B.E. 2558*. Bangkok.

c. Pension Benefits for Same-Sex Spouses

51.   Except for **New Zealand**, none of the analyzed countries have fully recognized marriage or civil partnerships of same-sex couples and therefore, do not extend employment benefits and pensions to same-sex spouses. In New Zealand, access to employment benefits and pension of same-sex spouses

---

[40] Magna Carta of Women (RA 9710 of 2009) of the Republic of the Philippines.
[41] Labor Code of Mongolia, 2021, Arts 6.1, 6.2, 6.6, 80.

is addressed in Sections 17–19 of the Superannuation and Retirement Income Act 2001, which explicitly calls for equal benefits for both same-sex and different-sex spouses.[42]

d.   Trans-Sensitive Regulations at the Workplace, including Gender-Neutral Facilities

52.   None of the countries have put in place laws and regulations that require employers to provide gender-neutral toilets and allow transgender employees to dress according to their gender identity. However, recently, in the **Philippines**, the Department of Social Welfare and Development issued a memo that called for respecting the right of transgender persons to wear a uniform that aligns with their gender identity (footnote 39).

2.   Recommendations

53.   Countries may consider adopting the following legal and policy practices to address SOGIESC-based discrimination in labor markets:

(i)   Enact legislation that provides comprehensive protections against SOGIESC-based discrimination during all stages of the employment process. Ensure existing anti-discriminatory laws and regulations for the labor market are harmonized and consistently used for sexual and gender minorities as well.

(ii)   Enact new legislation or amend existing labor laws to guarantee equal remuneration and benefits for work of equal value and protection from unfair dismissal to persons with diverse SOGIESC.

(iii) Enact legislation or regulations to establish an equality body or ombudsperson to receive and investigate complaints of SOGIESC-based discrimination at the workplace and provide remedies to victims of discrimination.

(iv)   Enact legislation or regulations to provide equal employment benefits and pension packages to diverse families.

(v)   Enact legislation or regulations that ensure standards and infrastructure to accommodate the specific needs of LGBTI employees, including establishing gender-neutral facilities.

54.   Additionally, countries may consider adopting the following practices to foster the inclusion of sexual and gender minorities:

(i)   Enact new legislation or amend existing labor laws to guarantee equal opportunities for on-the-job learning and training and career growth and advancement for sexual and gender minorities. Implement data collection interventions to understand the barriers LGBTI people experience in accessing and participating in labor markets effectively.

(ii)   Enact regulations to prohibit employers from asking questions or seeking information related to SOGIESC or the marital status of job applicants.

---

[42] New Zealand Superannuation and Retirement Income Act, 2001, Secs 17–19.

(iii)   Encourage employers to create an enabling environment for transgender employees regarding their transition by facilitating changes in internal personnel systems (such as name changes) and providing health insurance and paid leave for gender-affirming care.

(iv)   Introduce antidiscrimination and sensitization training programs in the workplace to create awareness among all employees about SOGIESC and implement broader public awareness campaigns to promote SOGIESC inclusion in the workplace and other domains of everyday life.

D. Access to Public Services and Social Protection

55.   This chapter focuses on access to health, housing, and social protection beyond the scope of education covered in the previous section.

56.   Equitable access to public services, such as health, housing, and social protection, is crucial to reducing and preventing poverty. Health and access to health care is a central concern for LGBTI people. Peer-reviewed research in Asia has demonstrated a causal relationship between the experience of stigma and discrimination and poor health outcomes, including depression, substance use, and suicide (footnote 6). Additional research shows high levels of discrimination by health care providers.[43]

57.   While the data on the impact of lack of access to public services and social protection (or lack thereof) on LGBTI people in Asia and the Pacific is scarce (Box 4), there is mounting evidence about the positive impact of these provisions on the health, economic, and education outcomes of

---

Box 4: Social Protection for LGBTI People—Lessons from COVID-19

Lesbian, gay, bisexual, transgender, and intersex (LGBTI) people across all countries in the Asia and Pacific region were one of the most adversely affected during the coronavirus disease (COVID-19) pandemic. Reasons include loss of employment opportunities during the lockdowns, precarious housing situation, increased vulnerability to family violence, lack of access to latest information on preventive measures, and lack of access to COVID-19 related health care and social protection measures due to systemic exclusion from public ID systems. Lessons learned from the COVID-19 experience can be applied to future programming on making public services and social protection more accessible and inclusive for LGBTI people. For example, universal access to essential health care services should be ensured for all and health care should be made affordable through public health insurance programs or health allowances for the most marginalized and financial vulnerable. Unemployment benefits should be extended to people working in informal labor markets. Rigid requirements around identity cards for social protection allowances for poorest population should be removed to ensure transgender people who lack legal gender recognition are able to access them. Governments should also provide subsidized or public housing to the poorest and financially vulnerable LGBTI people. Finally, governments should gather routine and systematic data on the impact of lack of social protection programs for LGBTI people.

Source: UN Independent Expert on Sexual Orientation and Gender Identity. 2020. ASPIRE Guidelines on COVID-19 response and recovery free from violence and discrimination based on sexual orientation and gender identity. A/HRC/75/258.

---

[43]   K. Fisk and J. Byrne. 2020. *The Cost of Stigma: Understanding and Addressing Health Implications of Transphobia and Discrimination on Transgender and Gender Diverse People. Evidence from a Trans-Led Research in Nepal, Indonesia, Thailand, and Vietnam.* Bangkok: APTN.

other marginalized population groups. For example, in the People's Republic of China, the Rural Pension Program has cut down dropout rates among girls.[44] In Pakistan, the Female Secondary School Stipend Program has increased enrollment rates among girls by 32% (footnote 45). In Viet Nam, over a third of disability allowance recipients have reported that it improves their access to medical care. Similar outcomes were documented in Nepal, where two-thirds of those receiving disability allowance indicated improved access to health care (footnote 45).

58.   Social protection programs have multiple components and can be adapted to the specific needs of a country's demographic and geographical contexts. For this study, we assessed:

(i)   Prohibition of SOGIESC-based discrimination in the provision of health care services, access to public housing and social protection, and access to public health insurance schemes for same-sex couples

(ii)   Inclusion of LGBTI people in the national census

(iii)   Legal recognition of transgender people and centralized protocols for change of gender markers without pathologizing

(iv)   Mechanisms for receiving complaints about SOGIESC-based discrimination in public services

1.   Findings

59.   Figure 4 presents the key findings of the study for this indicator set.

a   Antidiscrimination Laws and Regulations for Public Services and Social Protection, and Access to Public Health Insurance for Same-Sex Spouses

60.   None of the countries examined in the study have institutionalized antidiscrimination protections for sexual and gender minorities in relation to access to public services and social protection. However, some countries have enacted legal provisions that call for nondiscrimination in health care settings. For example, **Fiji**'s Constitution contains a broad antidiscrimination provision for sexual and gender minorities. Further, Article 38 of Fiji's Constitution establishes the Right to Health for all.[45] Article 6 of **Georgia**'s Law on Healthcare, 1997, establishes the nondiscrimination principle in relation to access to health care for persons with diverse sexual orientations. However, the law does not provide these protections for trans and gender-diverse persons and intersex persons.

61.   National Human Rights Commission Act of the **Republic of Korea** 2009, prohibits nondiscrimination based on "sexual inclination" for access to goods and services, including housing and access to land.[46] The provision applies to health care services as well. However, it is important to note that the recommendations of the National Human Rights Commission are not legally binding, which weakens the protections outlined in the act. While the legislative instruments in the Republic of Korea

---

[44]   UN ESCAP. 2018. Why We Need Social Protection. *Social Development Policy Guides*. Bangkok: UN ESCAP.

[45]   Constitution of Fiji, 2013, Sec. 38.

[46]   National Human Rights Commission Act of the Republic of Korea, 2009, Art. 2.

Figure 4: Access to Public Services and Social Protection

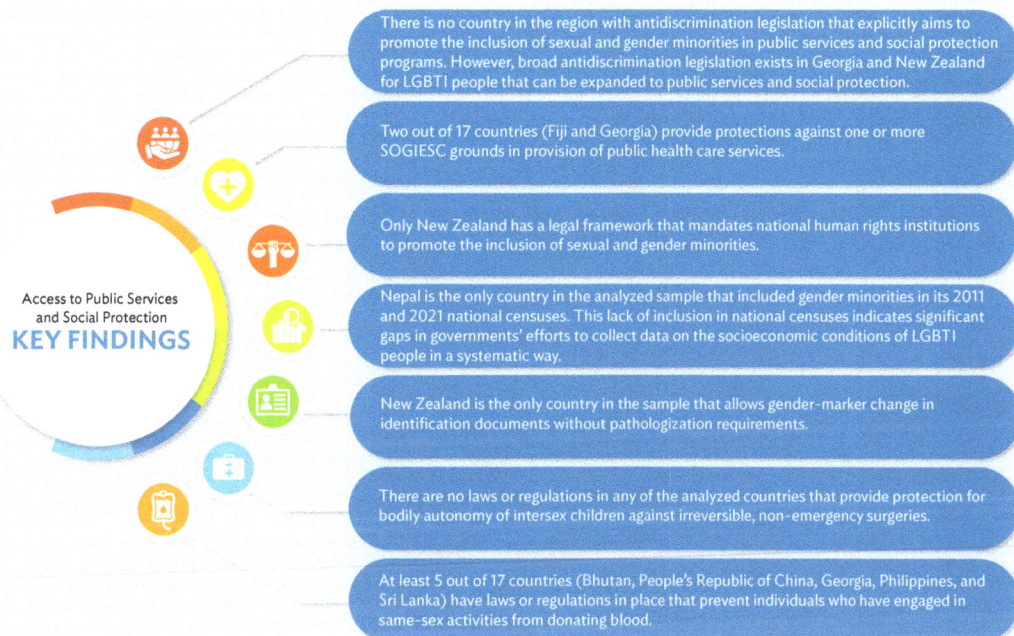

Access to Public Services and Social Protection
KEY FINDINGS

There is no country in the region with antidiscrimination legislation that explicitly aims to promote the inclusion of sexual and gender minorities in public services and social protection programs. However, broad antidiscrimination legislation exists in Georgia and New Zealand for LGBTI people that can be expanded to public services and social protection.

Two out of 17 countries (Fiji and Georgia) provide protections against one or more SOGIESC grounds in provision of public health care services.

Only New Zealand has a legal framework that mandates national human rights institutions to promote the inclusion of sexual and gender minorities.

Nepal is the only country in the analyzed sample that included gender minorities in its 2011 and 2021 national censuses. This lack of inclusion in national censuses indicates significant gaps in governments' efforts to collect data on the socioeconomic conditions of LGBTI people in a systematic way.

New Zealand is the only country in the sample that allows gender-marker change in identification documents without pathologization requirements.

There are no laws or regulations in any of the analyzed countries that provide protection for bodily autonomy of intersex children against irreversible, non-emergency surgeries.

At least 5 out of 17 countries (Bhutan, People's Republic of China, Georgia, Philippines, and Sri Lanka) have laws or regulations in place that prevent individuals who have engaged in same-sex activities from donating blood.

LGBTI = lesbian, gay, bisexual, transgender, and intersex; SOGIESC = sexual orientation, gender identity and expression, and sex characteristics.
Source: Asian Development Bank.

are silent on the provision of public health insurance to same-sex couples, most recently, a local court has ruled that same-sex couples should be granted the same access to public health insurance benefits as different-sex couples. This set a significant precedent for upholding the right to nondiscrimination and equality and for amplifying antidiscrimination advocacy.

b.   Inclusion of LGBTI People in National Censuses

62.   Systemic and disaggregated data on the social and economic characteristics of LGBTI people are necessary to inform and influence laws, regulations, and policies (Box 5). Yet efforts to collect disaggregated data for sexual and gender minorities have remained limited, owing to systemic barriers. Of the analyzed countries, in 2011 **Nepal** became the first country to include a third gender in its census and is currently the only country in the analyzed sample that has included a third gender category. However, there have been limitations in its implementation, for administrative and logistical reasons.

63.   **New Zealand** has announced that its 2023 national census will include sexual and gender minorities in the surveys to expand the country's data collection efforts to understand the specific needs of these communities.[47]

---

[47]   RNZ. 2020. Gender, Sexual Identity Added to Census: "We're Trying to Do Right." *The New Zealand Herald*. 2 November.

**Box 5: Lack of Inclusion of Sexual and Gender Minorities
in Data Collection Efforts and Its Impact**

"Ultimately, lack of data about LGBT persons renders the community invisible to policymakers and government duty-bearers and will reinforce patterns of negation and the adoption of irrational State policies. In the context of negation, perpetrators feel motivated and enabled to suppress or punish diversity. So even where States collect data, negation can result in information that is unreliable, unsystematic and biased."

LGBT = lesbian, gay, bisexual, transgender, and intersex.
Source: UN Independent Expert on Sexual Orientation and Gender Identity (SOGI). 2019. Data Collection and Management as a Means to Create Heightened Awareness of Violence and Discrimination Based on Sexual Orientation and Gender Identity. A/HRC/41/45.

---

c.   Legal Gender Recognition

64.   The lack of legal gender recognition poses a critical barrier for transgender and gender-diverse persons in accessing public services and benefiting from social protection. For example, there is mounting evidence that the lack of legal gender recognition systematically barred transgender and gender-diverse persons from accessing coronavirus disease (COVID-19)-related relief and recovery programs across the Asia and Pacific region.[48] Further, the lack of legal gender recognition also poses a barrier to recognition and equality before the law and access to equal protections and entitlements (Box 6).[49]

Box 6: Misgendering of Transgender Students in Educational Institutions

In Nepal, a transwoman was prohibited from taking university exams because of discrepancies in name and gender marker in her current legal identification documents and the school transcripts that were issued before her transition. Misgendering in official documents causes systemic hurdles for transgender students in enrolling in educational institutions.

Source: A. Ghimire. 2023. Tribhuvan University System Doesn't Recognise Transgender Student. *The Kathmandu Post*. 9 June.

---

65.   Despite increasing evidence on the correlation between legal gender recognition and socioeconomic development and inclusion of trans and gender-diverse people,[50] a majority of the countries in the Asia and Pacific region have not enacted specific legislation to allow for legal gender recognition on a self-identification basis. **New Zealand** is the only country in the analyzed sample that has enacted a law that allows for a gender change on identification documents on a self-identification

---

[48]   Edge Effect. 2021. "We Don't Do A Lot For Them Specifically": A Scoping Report on Gaps and Opportunities for Improving Diverse SOGIESC Inclusion in Cash Transfer and Social Protection Programs, during the COVID-19 Crisis and Beyond. Report for the Australian Department of Foreign Affairs and Trade.

[49]   United Nations Independent Expert on SOGI. 2018. Report on Legal Recognition of Gender and Depathologization. A/73/152.

[50]   UNDP and APTN. 2017. Legal Gender Recognition: A Multi-Country Legal and Policy Review in Asia. Bangkok.

basis.[51] **Nepal** has provided constitutional rights to transgender persons to change the gender marker on a self-identification basis to reflect their third gender on citizenship certificates and passports; however, Nepal does not allow transwomen to change their gender marker to "female," and transmen to change their gender marker to "male."[52]

66.   In Southeast Asia, **Viet Nam** passed an amendment in its Civil Code in 2015 by including Article 37, which clearly states that an individual will be allowed to change their gender on identity documents by law.[53] However, the country has yet to issue policy directives or protocols to implement the amendment. A draft Law on Gender Affirmation has been developed by local activists and academics that provides detailed protocols for legal gender recognition based on standards outlined by international human rights frameworks. Viet Nam's National Assembly Standing Committee has accepted the draft. If the National Assembly agrees, the draft law will be discussed during its session in October 2024 and voted on in the May 2025 session.[54] Similar efforts are underway in the **Philippines,** where an Antidiscrimination Bill or SOGIE Equality Bill is currently being reviewed by the Senate.

67.   The majority of the countries analyzed only allow for gender marker changes after either a sex reassignment surgery or after receiving a medical note on gender dysphoria (Table 5).

Table 5: Examples of Pathologizing Requirements for a Gender Marker Change in ID/Passport

Country	Pathologizing Requirements
Bhutan	Requires recommendations from civil society organizations and a medical note to allow for gender marker changes in legal identification documents.
People's Republic of China	Requires completion of gender-affirming surgeries for gender marker changes in legal identification documents.
Republic of Korea	Requires either a medical professional's certificate or completion of gender-affirming surgeries for gender marker changes. However, several district courts have allowed a change of gender marker in identification documents without requiring the completion of gender-affirming surgeries.[a]

[a] Amnesty International. 2019. *Serving in Silence: LGBTI People in South Korea's Military*. London: Amnesty International.
Source: Compiled by authors.

68.   Some countries in the region have taken a step back on legal gender recognition. For example, Mongolia amended its Law on Civil State Registration in 2018 to include a provision for gender marker change based on medical verification that the individual has gone through a "full" transition, including through gender-affirming surgery.[55] Prior to this, Mongolia required a medical diagnosis of gender dysphoria; in that sense, Mongolia has added more stringent requirements to allow for gender marker change, and the 2018 amendment is a step back in terms of legal reform on this issue.

[51]   Births, Deaths, Marriages and Relationships Registration Act of New Zealand, 2021.

[52]   Constitution of Nepal, 2075 (2015), Art. 12.

[53]   Civil Code of Viet Nam, 2015, Art. 37.

[54]   R. IJsendijk. 2023. Eight Years and Counting: Why the Gender Affirmation Law Matters in Viet Nam. UNDP. 16 May.

[55]   Law on Civil State Registration of Mongolia, 2018.

69.   On 1 August 2020, amendments to the Law of the Kyrgyz Republic "On Acts of Civil Status" came into effect, in which provisions for legal gender recognition were removed.[56] After this amendment, trans people were denied legal gender recognition by civil registry offices, and they were unable to change their gender marker in identity documents. The amendment was appealed in the Constitutional Court of the Kyrgyz Republic; however, the court rejected the claim that the lack of legal gender recognition was discrimination.

70.   In **Thailand,** the Department of Women's Affairs and Family Development collaborated with local transgender rights groups and Thammasat University to draft a Gender Recognition Bill. However, local transgender rights groups criticized the bill heavily as it did not include many of their recommendations for legal gender recognition bill. Currently, Thailand does not have legal gender recognition and has not adopted the World Health Organization's latest International Classification of Diseases, 11th Revision (ICD-11). Therefore, anyone wishing to undergo gender-affirming surgeries is required to obtain a psychiatric assessment for gender dysphoria as a precondition. A new draft of the Gender Recognition Bill has been prepared and is ready for submission to the Cabinet.

d.   Establishment of National Human Rights Institutions to Ensure Nondiscrimination and Advance LGBTI Inclusion

71.   **Fiji** and **New Zealand** are the only countries that mandate their national human rights institution by law to promote the inclusion of sexual minorities and ensure nondiscrimination based on a person's sexual orientation. New Zealand's Human Rights Act 1993 establishes the principle of nondiscrimination across various sectors and applies this principle to several social protection initiatives established by the New Zealand Superannuation and Retirement Income Act 2001.[57] In Fiji, Section 45 of the Constitution mandates the Fiji Human Rights and Anti-Discrimination Commission to promote the principle of nondiscrimination as established by the Constitution and to receive and investigate claims of discrimination from persons with diverse sexual orientations and gender identities and make recommendations for remedy and redressal.

72.   Additionally, in Nepal, a focal person has been appointed by the National Human Rights Commission to promote the inclusion of LGBTI people in the strategic priorities of the commission. In the Philippines, the Commission on Human Rights is designated the gender ombudsperson under the Magna Carta of Women (footnote 40). In this role, it is mandated to advance and protect the rights of women and sexual and gender minorities.

2.   Recommendations

73.   Countries may consider adopting the following legal and policy practices to address the gaps in the current legislative framework and to ensure equal access to public services and social protection for sexual and gender minorities:

---

[56]   Law of the Kyrgyz Republic "On Acts of Civil Status" (Law No. 110), 2020, Art. 35.

[57]   New Zealand's Human Rights Act, Secs 53 and 70.

(i)   Enact comprehensive antidiscrimination legislation to prohibit SOGIESC-based discrimination in public services and social protection, including health care, social housing, public health insurance programs, social protection for persons with disabilities, and old age social security. Countries should expand the legal interpretation of existing nondiscrimination laws, including constitutional provisions, prohibiting SOGIESC discrimination.

(ii)   Amend existing laws and regulations to extend social protection benefits to LGBTI families, including public health insurance.

(iii)   Implement initiatives to collect data on the socioeconomic and development status and patterns of sexual and gender minorities, including through inclusion in the national census, wherever possible. In doing so, ensure these efforts are guided by the "do no harm" principle.[58] Additionally, building on lessons learned from the experiences of those countries that have included sexual and gender minorities in their census, data collection methodologies (e.g., household surveys, individual surveys, among others) should be amended to make them more accurate, contextually sensitive, and relevant.

(iv)   Enact laws and regulations to allow legal gender recognition on a self-identification basis, without needing psychiatric assessments, sterilization, and/or gender reassignment surgery, and establish protocols to facilitate the issuance of new ID documents or amendments of existing ID documents without bureaucratic hurdles.

(v)   Amend existing laws and regulations and enact new pieces of legislation, where applicable, to mandate national human rights institutions to review laws and policies and make recommendations to the government to promote the inclusion of sexual and gender minorities and to receive and investigate complaints of SOGIESC-based discrimination and provide redressal to victims of such discrimination.

74.   Additionally, to support the enforcement of laws that promote access to public services and social protection of sexual and gender minorities, countries may adopt the following good practices:

(i)   Implement SOGIESC-inclusivity training for public service professionals to address biases and misconceptions about LGBTI people. The government should also implement public awareness campaigns to combat bias and discrimination based on SOGIESC status in providing goods and services.

E. Civil and Political Inclusion

75.   Civil and political inclusion refers to, among others, the legal recognition of same-sex unions, freedom of association and expression for sexual and gender minorities, inclusion of sexual and gender minorities in the countries' development plans and strategies, and inclusion of LGBTI people in the political and legislative spaces.

---

[58]   Researchers and organizations that collect data on LGBTI individuals should do so considering the risks posed to all stakeholders, including sexual and gender minorities, at all stages. Data should be used responsibly and ethically. Data should be reported accurately and used to advance understanding, advocate for positive change, and address disparities or social inequalities.

76.   This indicator set measures the extent to which legal instruments of analyzed countries promote the inclusion of LGBTI people in the social and political fabric. It also measures efforts toward the de-stigmatization of diverse sexual orientations and gender identities, including through removing diverse SOGIESCs from the list of mental disorders. The indicator set also looks at laws and regulations that aim to protect individuals who are seeking asylum on the basis of fear of persecution owing to their SOGIESC. Further, laws and regulations related to the prevention of the so-called "conversion therapies" are also measured under this indicator. More specifically, this indicator set looks at:

(i)   Number of national, elected representatives, cabinet members, and supreme court justices who openly self-identify as a sexual or gender minority or intersex

(ii)   National action plans for LGTBI inclusion

(iii)   Civil participation and freedom of association for LGBTI people

(iv)   Recognition of same-sex unions and marriages (including from other countries)

(v)   Adoption rights for same-sex couples and equal access to assisted reproductive technology

(vi)   Prohibition of "conversion practices"

(vii)   Protections for intersex children against irreversible, non-emergency surgeries

(viii)   Classification of being homo/bisexual, transgender, or intersex as a mental or physical disorder

(ix)   Recognition of SOGIESC-based persecution as grounds for asylum

1.   Findings

77.   Figure 5 presents the findings of this study for this indicator.

a.   Inclusion of LGBTI Leaders in Civic and Political Spaces

78.   Most of the analyzed countries in the region lack positive legislation and regulations that promote civil and political inclusion of sexual and gender minorities. This could be a reason why, of the 17 analyzed countries, only **New Zealand**, the **Philippines**, and **Thailand** have a member of parliament or a judge of the country's court who self-identifies as belonging to a sexual and/or gender minority.

b.   National Action Plans for LGBTI Inclusion

79.   The majority of the analyzed countries do not have any national action plans or development strategies to promote the inclusion of LGBTI people. **Nepal** adopted a National Human Rights Action Plan in 2020, which outlined the elimination of "social discrimination against sexual and gender minorities" as one of the strategic priorities of the government.[59] **Thailand**'s 4th National Human Rights Action Plan (2019–2022) resulted in several sub-plans, including one focusing on the promotion of the

---

59   National Human Rights Action Plan of Nepal, 2020.

Figure 5: Civil and Political Inclusion

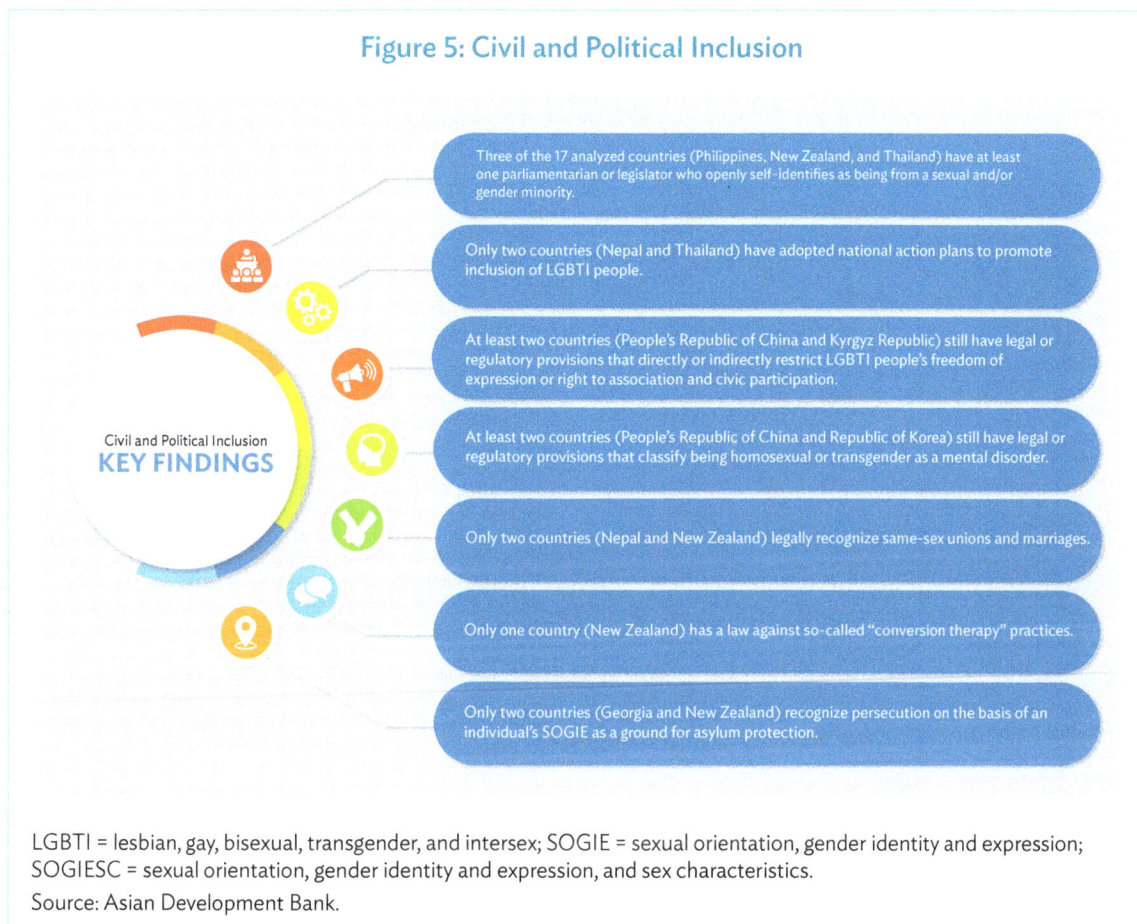

Civil and Political Inclusion
KEY FINDINGS

Three of the 17 analyzed countries (Philippines, New Zealand, and Thailand) have at least one parliamentarian or legislator who openly self-identifies as being from a sexual and/or gender minority.

Only two countries (Nepal and Thailand) have adopted national action plans to promote inclusion of LGBTI people.

At least two countries (People's Republic of China and Kyrgyz Republic) still have legal or regulatory provisions that directly or indirectly restrict LGBTI people's freedom of expression or right to association and civic participation.

At least two countries (People's Republic of China and Republic of Korea) still have legal or regulatory provisions that classify being homosexual or transgender as a mental disorder.

Only two countries (Nepal and New Zealand) legally recognize same-sex unions and marriages.

Only one country (New Zealand) has a law against so-called "conversion therapy" practices.

Only two countries (Georgia and New Zealand) recognize persecution on the basis of an individual's SOGIE as a ground for asylum protection.

LGBTI = lesbian, gay, bisexual, transgender, and intersex; SOGIE = sexual orientation, gender identity and expression; SOGIESC = sexual orientation, gender identity and expression, and sex characteristics.
Source: Asian Development Bank.

human rights of LGBT people.[60] In **Cambodia**[61] and **Timor-Leste,**[62] violence against LGBTI people has been addressed in their national action plans on gender-based violence.

c. Civil Participation and Freedom of Association of LGBTI People

80.   CSOs play a critical role in promoting the inclusion of sexual and gender minorities and increasing their access to health care and other services that are often a part of the public services realm. An enabling legal environment is crucial for CSOs to operate their functions effectively and to reach out to marginalized population groups, including sexual and gender minorities. Except for **PNG**, all analyzed countries allow registration and operation of LGBTI organizations. PNG has legislation that allows the denial of registration of a charity or nonprofit organization on moral grounds.[63] In the **Kyrgyz Republic**, the relevant law is silent on the registration of LGBTI organizations; however, several LGBTI organizations are openly operating in the country.

---

[60] 4th National Human Rights Action Plan of Thailand (2019–2022).

[61] The National Plan of Action to End Violence Against Women (2019 to 2023), Cambodia.

[62] The National Plan of Action on Gender Based Violence (2017–2021), Timor-Leste.

[63] Associations Incorporation Act of Papua New Guinea, 1966, Sec. 4.1.

81.   Sexual and gender minorities in several analyzed countries experience various forms of barriers to fully exercising their right to freedom of expression and association. These barriers range from explicit legal restrictions to freely and openly discussing issues related to sexuality and gender to administrative hurdles to forming LGBTI groups. For example, Article 10 of the Constitution of the **Kyrgyz Republic** allows for indirect censorship of any LGBTI inclusion-related events and information as they may be deemed contrary to "moral values and the public consciousness of the people of Kyrgyzstan." Additionally, the Kyrgyz Republic has enacted a law similar to LGBTI propaganda laws across Eastern Europe and the Russian Federation (Box 7).[64]

> ## Box 7: Law "On Measures to Prevent Harm to Children's Health, Physical, Intellectual, Mental, Spiritual and Moral Development in the Kyrgyz Republic" 2023
>
> In 2014, a draft law to criminalize "fostering positive attitude" toward "non-traditional sexual relations" (the "LGBTI propaganda" law) was introduced into the Parliament of the Kyrgyz Republic. Under the draft law, any positive or neutral reference to "non-traditional sexual relations" in public or the media would be banned, as would any public assemblies promoting LGBTI issues. The draft law received support from the majority in the parliament; however, discussions on the bill halted. In recent years, discussions on the passage of the bill reemerged in the context of the rise of anti-gay propaganda legislation in several former Soviet Union countries, and in August 2023 the law "On Measures to Prevent Harm to Children's Health, Physical, Intellectual, Mental, Spiritual and Moral Development in the Kyrgyz Republic" was formally enacted. The law prohibits any public depiction or discussion of "non-tradition sexual relations."
>
> LGBTI = lesbian, gay, bisexual, transexual, and intersex.
> Source: On Measures to Prevent Harm to Children's Health, Physical, Intellectual, Mental, Spiritual and Moral Development in the Kyrgyz Republic, 2023, Art. 2(1).

d.   Legalization of Same-Sex Marriage and Unions, Adoption Rights, and Access to Human-Assisted Reproductive Technology for Same-Sex Couples

82.   Except for **New Zealand**, none of the analyzed countries in the region legally recognize any form of same-sex union or same-sex marriage. In New Zealand, same-sex marriages and unions are legally recognized through the Marriage Amendment Act 2013[65] and the Civil Union Act 2004.[66] New Zealand also grants adoption or joint parenting options for same-sex couples. Further, the country's legislation on human-assisted reproductive technology (ART) does not discriminate against same-sex couples.

83.   Countires in Southeast and South Asia are inching closer to legally recognizing same-sex partnerships. In June 2022, **Thailand**'s Cabinet passed a reading of four bills that proposed legalizing same-sex unions or partnerships;[67] however, the review process will start again after the upcoming elections, and the bill will be submitted to the new cabinet for review and approval. In August 2022, a bill that proposed the legalization of same-sex unions was presented in the **Philippines'** Senate. However,

---

[64]   Constitution of the Kyrgyz Republic, 2021, Art. 10.

[65]   Marriage (Definition of Marriage) Amendment Act of New Zealand, 2013.

[66]   Civil Union Act of New Zealand, 2004.

[67]   *Reuters*. 2022. Thailand Edges Closer to Legalising Same-Sex Unions. 16 June.

there has not been any further development on this issue since then. In **Viet Nam**, an amendment was enacted in 2014 to the Law on Marriage and Family that removed a ban on same-sex marriages (Article 10[5]), replacing it with a provision that states that the state does not legally recognize same-sex marriages (Article 8, provision 2). In June 2023, **Nepal**'s Supreme Court ordered the government to establish mechanisms to register same-sex marriages without requiring new legislation. Earlier in December 2022, Nepal's Supreme Court ordered the government to grant legal recognition to a foreign same-sex spouse of a Nepalese citizen.[68]

e.   Banning So-Called "Conversion Therapy"

84.   **New Zealand** is the only country in the region and one of the handful of countries in the world that have outlawed so-called "conversion therapy" practices against sexual and gender minorities. New Zealand has enacted the Conversion Practices Prohibition Legislation Act 2022, which provides comprehensive legal protections against various forms of conversion practices aimed at sexual and gender minorities and calls for "open and respectful discussion regarding sexuality and gender."[69] Previously, New Zealand enacted the Human Rights Act 1993, which also legally prohibited conversion therapy.

85.   Despite the so-called conversion therapy practices being prevalent in the region (Box 8), very few countries have enacted explicit legislation to eradicate it.

Box 8: Examples of Conversion Therapy Practices in Sri Lanka

According to a study conducted by the Asia Pacifc Transgender Network (APTN) in Sri Lanka, multiple forms of "conversion therapies" are offered by practitioners of both indigenous (Ayurvedic) medicine and western medicine. These involve the administration of medication and shock therapy. Additionally, perpetrators of "conversion therapies" in the medical sector face next to no repercussions because there are no monitoring mechanisms and regulatory guidelines that discourage and ban the so-called "conversion therapy."

Source: C. Weerawardhana. 2021. Conversion Therapy Practices in Sri Lanka: Country Profile. APTN.

f.   Ensuring Protection for Intersex Children

86.   An estimated 1.7% of children in the world every year are born with variations in their sex characteristics. Many of these children undergo surgeries to "normalize" their sex characteristics and gender appearances. These surgeries are irreversible and invasive and are conducted without the consent of intersex children. These surgeries are not medically necessary and are a gross violation of intersex children's human right to bodily autonomy and integrity. Intersex people across the world have started to speak out against these surgeries and have urged governments to put in place legal safeguards against these invasive, nonconsensual medical procedures that have a profound impact on them.[70]

---

[68]   Adheep Pokhrel et al. vs Ministry of Home Affairs (Supreme Court of Nepal, December 2022).

[69]   Conversion Practices Prohibition Legislation Act of New Zealand, 2022.

[70]   HRW and InterAct: Advocates for Intersex Youth. 2017. "I Want to Be Like Nature Made Me": Medically Unnecessary Surgeries on Intersex Children in the US. New York: HRW.

87.   None of the analyzed countries have put in place legal or regulatory protections against these surgeries. At the same time, none of the analyzed countries in the region have laws or regulations that require intersex children to undergo "corrective" surgeries to receive a birth certificate. In **New Zealand**, there is an option of "I/indeterminate" in the birth certificate for the sex of a newborn.

g.   Classifying Homosexuality and Being Transgender as Mental Disorders

88.   **Viet Nam**'s Ministry of Health has public directives that state that homosexuality and being transgender are not mental illnesses, and therefore "cannot be 'cured' nor need[s] to be 'cured' and cannot be converted in any way."[71] While the country has no legislation against pathologizing diverse gender identities or conversion practices, the directive is a significant step toward aligning its legislative and policy frameworks with international best practices and standards.

89.   Additionally, gradual progress toward the de-pathologization of homosexuality and transgender people has been observed across all countries. The World Health Organization (WHO) has advocated for the removal of the existing classification of "gender identity disorder" and its replacement with "gender incongruence of adolescence and adulthood" in ICD-11.[72] However, the adoption of these recommendations and definitions varies across the region.

90.   In the **Republic of Korea,** the Military Service Physical Examination Rule 2021 categorizes "gender incongruence" as a type of mental disorder (Article 12).[73]

91.   In **Armenia**, revealing a person's sexual orientation during conscription could lead to exemption from compulsory military services followed by a medical assessment as they are diagnosed with having a mental disorder. Consequently, this diagnosis becomes a permanent part of their medical record, significantly impeding various aspects of their lives, such as their ability to pursue certain professions. This diagnosis is also included in their health records in the new digital health system. The information in the digital health records is made available to any medical professional who will treat the person in the future, violating their privacy and confidentiality and increasing the risk of being refused treatment based on sexual orientation and gender identity (SOGI).[74]

h.   Recognition of Persecution on the Basis of SOGIESC as Grounds for Asylum

92.   **Georgia** provides explicit legal protections to LGBTI people who are facing persecution as a result of their SOGIESC status so they can seek asylum.[75] New Zealand's Refugee Status Appeal Authority has granted asylum based on the sexual orientation of the asylum-seeker.[76]

---

[71] Ministry of Health, Vietnam, Directive No. 4132/BYT-PC.

[72] WHO's ICD-11 is the latest international standard to establish comparability on the classification of diseases.

[73] Military Service Physical Examination Rule of Republic of Korea, 2021, Art. 12 and Annex. 3.

[74] Decree of the Ministry of Health of Armenia, 2018, Art. 8; ECOM, New Generation Humanitarian NGO, and National Trans Coalition NGO. 2023. *Joint Submission to the United Nations Committee on Economic, Social and Cultural Rights ahead of the Consideration of Armenia's Fourth Periodic Report at the 74th Session*; Chaikhana. 2022. *Armenia's Silent Agreement: Homophobia in the Military*. 20 September.

[75] Law of Georgia on International Protection, 2016, Arts 8 and 10.

[76] Refugee Appeal No. 1312/93, Refugee Status Appeals Authority New Zealand.

2.   Recommendations

93.   Countries may consider adopting the following legal and policy practices to address the gaps in the existing legal framework and to foster inclusion of sexual and gender minorities:

(i)   Establish inclusive legal and regulatory instruments that foster political participation of sexual and gender minorities.

(ii)   Adopt comprehensive national action plans focusing on antidiscrimination efforts and protecting sexual and gender minorities.

(iii)   Amend existing laws and regulations to ensure that LGBTI CSOs can operate their functions freely and receive funding to support their operations.

(iv)   Enact laws to ban and penalize conversion therapy of sexual and gender minorities.

(v)   Enact laws and regulations to ban irreversible surgeries on intersex children and put in place regulations to allow their birth registration as "intersex."

(vi)   Abolish medical professional classifications that pathologize homosexuality and trans and gender-diverse identities and ensure national clinical classifications are in line with WHO's ICD-11.

(vii)   Introduce legislation or amend existing legal instruments to recognize persecution based on SOGIESC as grounds for asylum.

94.   Additionally, countries may consider adopting the following practices to foster the inclusion of sexual and gender minorities in civil and political spaces:

(i)   Implement public campaigns to raise public awareness about SOGIESC and to address existing myths and social biases against LGBTI people.

F. Protection from Hate Crimes

95.   SOGIESC-based hate crimes are motivated by prejudice based on a person's actual or perceived sexual orientation, gender identity and expressions, and sex characteristics and can range from insults and hate speech to psychological attacks (threats and intimidation) and physical violence.[77] In addition to suffering individual attacks or street crimes, LGBTI people have been a target of more organized hate crimes by religious organizations and far-right groups. A study conducted in the United States has also reported that hate crimes against LGBTI people are often of a higher degree of violence and brutality.[78] This is especially true for lesbian and bisexual women across the Asia and Pacific region, who have reported experiencing assaults and attacks of sexual nature.[79] At the same time,

---

[77]   ILGA Europe. 2023. Annual Review of Human Rights Situation of LGBTI People in Europe and Central Asia.

[78]   A. R. Flores et al. 2022. Hate Crimes against LGBT People: National Crime Victimization Survey, 2017–2019. PLOS ONE 17(12).

[79]   Outright International. 2014. *Violence: Through the Lens of Lesbian and Bisexual Women and Trans People in Asia.* Outright International: New York.

SOGIESC-based hate crimes remain underreported as there are no formal mechanisms for reporting or monitoring hate crimes.[80] Lesbian and bisexual women who are victims of SOGIESC-based hate crimes have also reported experiencing revictimization when they have attempted to report violent assaults, owing to prevalent patriarchal norms (footnote 79). Lesbian and bisexual women victims of SOGIESC-based hate crimes have also reported not filing complaints against assaults because the perpetrators are often their family members (footnote 79). This indicator set looks at:

(i)   Criminalization of SOGIESC-based hate crimes (including aggravated circumstances)

(ii)   Mandatory data collection by government bodies on SOGIESC-based hate crimes

(iii) Mechanisms to monitor and report SOGIESC-based hate crimes

(iv)   Mandatory training of the police, the judiciary, and other relevant authorities on recognizing and identifying SOGIESC-based hate crimes and provision of services for victims

1.   Findings

96.   Figure 6 presents the key findings for this indicator set.

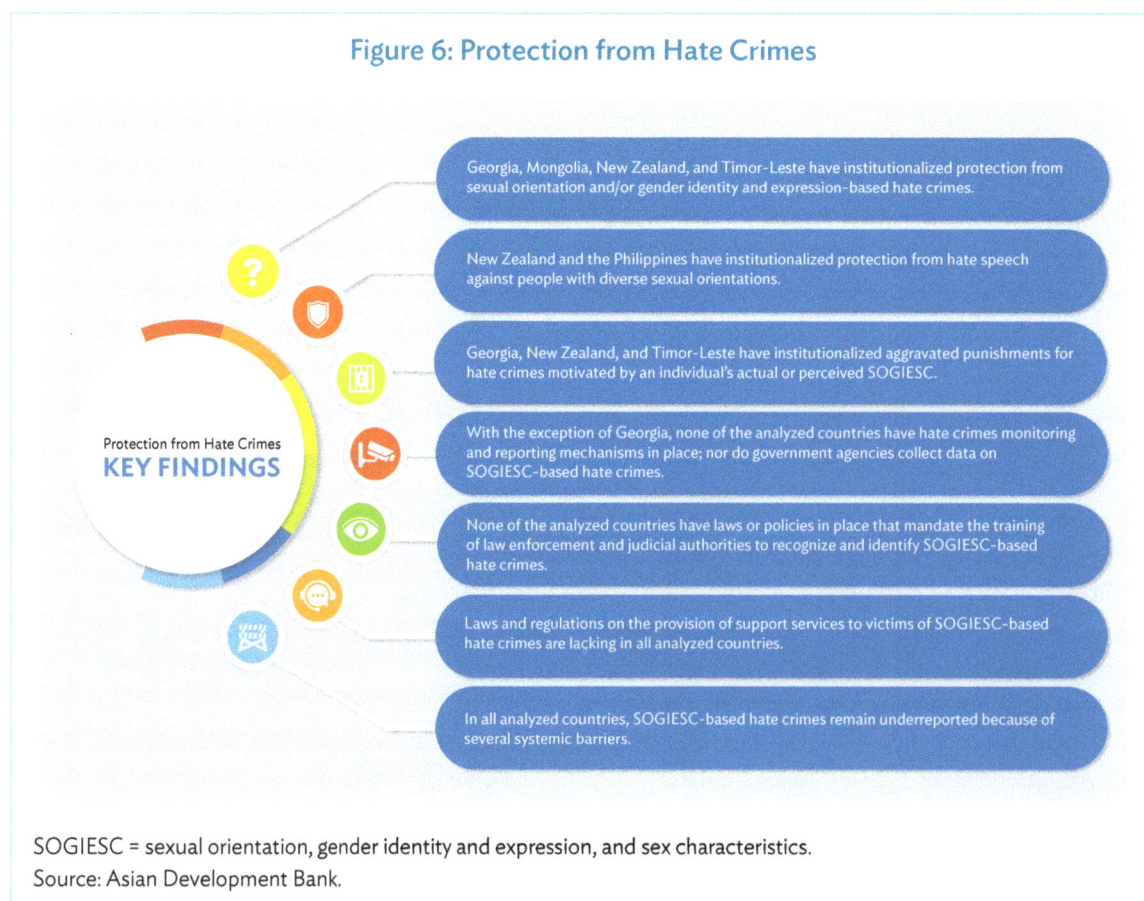

Figure 6: Protection from Hate Crimes

Protection from Hate Crimes
KEY FINDINGS

Georgia, Mongolia, New Zealand, and Timor-Leste have institutionalized protection from sexual orientation and/or gender identity and expression-based hate crimes.

New Zealand and the Philippines have institutionalized protection from hate speech against people with diverse sexual orientations.

Georgia, New Zealand, and Timor-Leste have institutionalized aggravated punishments for hate crimes motivated by an individual's actual or perceived SOGIESC.

With the exception of Georgia, none of the analyzed countries have hate crimes monitoring and reporting mechanisms in place; nor do government agencies collect data on SOGIESC-based hate crimes.

None of the analyzed countries have laws or policies in place that mandate the training of law enforcement and judicial authorities to recognize and identify SOGIESC-based hate crimes.

Laws and regulations on the provision of support services to victims of SOGIESC-based hate crimes are lacking in all analyzed countries.

In all analyzed countries, SOGIESC-based hate crimes remain underreported because of several systemic barriers.

SOGIESC = sexual orientation, gender identity and expression, and sex characteristics.
Source: Asian Development Bank.

---

[80] As reported by the expert contributors ADB consulted for this study.

a. Criminalization of SOGIESC-Based Hate Crimes

97. Only four out of 17 analyzed countries have legal protections of varying degrees against sexual orientation and gender identity-based hate crimes (Table 6).

Table 6: Examples of Good Practices in Protection from Hate Crimes

Country	Measure
Georgia	Art. 53(3) of the Criminal Code criminalizes hate crimes motivated by sexual orientation and gender identity, among other grounds. The provision also establishes these grounds as aggravated circumstances.[a]
Mongolia	Art. 10 of the Criminal Code 2015 criminalizes murders motivated by sexual orientation-related prejudice or hatred and establishes it as an aggravated circumstance with a more severe punishment.
New Zealand	New Zealand establishes hostility toward sexual orientation and gender identity as aggravating circumstances for crimes under the Sentencing Act 2002.[c]
Timor-Leste	Decree Law No. 19/2009 Approves the Penal Code,2009 Art. 52 establishes hate crimes motivated by sexual orientation as a "higher level of unlawfulness" with aggravated penalties.[d]

[a] Criminal Code of Georgia, 1999, Art. 53(3).
[b] Criminal Code of Mongolia, 2015, Art. 10.
[c] Sentencing Act of New Zealand, 2002, Sec. 9(1)(h).
[d] Penal Code of Timor-Leste, 2009, Art. 52.

Source: Compiled by authors.

98. In the **Philippines**, hate speech, including transphobic and homophobic slurs and remarks, verbal or in writing, is prohibited under the Safe Spaces Act 2019. Similarly, **New Zealand**'s Harmful Digital Communications Act 2015 establishes that digital communication should not denigrate a person based on their sexual orientation.[81]

99. Further, in response to a communication from the United Nations Independent Expert on SOGI, the Government of the **Republic of Korea** stated that "based on the Rules on Broadcast Review (Rules No. 123 of Korea Communications Standards Commission) in accordance with Art. 33 of the Broadcast Law, the Commission reviews expressions and statements on broadcast media that show hatred against or that caricatures, mocks, or degrades sexual minorities" to ensure that media broadcasters abide by relevant regulations. [82] However, the provisions do not explicitly address SOGIESC-based hate speech.

b. Data Collection and Monitoring of SOGIESC-Based Hate Crimes

100. Except for **Georgia**, in all analyzed countries, there are no reporting or monitoring mechanisms for SOGIESC-based hate crimes. Georgia established a Human Rights Protection and Monitoring Department in the Ministry of International Affairs in 2018 to monitor hate crimes, collect statistics, and oversee the initial stage of investigation on other ordinary crimes motivated by bias. There are two mechanisms used for case monitoring: one is an internal control mechanism, which employs an electronic platform for investigation conducted by the employees of the Department on a daily basis,

---

[81] Harmful Digital Communications Act of New Zealand, 2015, Sec. 6.
[82] Response of the Government of the Republic of Korea to Communication issued by the UN Independent Expert on SOGI on 5 April 2018.

and the other is an external mechanism, which entails receiving information on particular incidents and cases from external actors such as nongovernmental and other organizations, be it in written or verbal form. An email account has been set up to serve these purposes. Bias motivations listed in Paragraph 3(1) of Article 53 of the Criminal Code of Georgia, including sexual orientation, are then monitored.

101.   However, there are national and international CSOs and community groups that are collecting and publishing data on transphobic and homophobic crimes in all sample countries. Further, in the **Republic of Korea**, the National Human Rights Commission conducts research on the prevalence of hate speech against sexual and gender minorities and women in online spaces.

c.   Training of Police and Prosecutors and Provision of Support Services for Victims

102.   In all analyzed countries, there are no laws or regulations that mandate the training of police authorities, judicial officials, and medical professionals to manage cases of SOGIESC-based hate crimes in a victim-sensitive manner. There are also no laws or regulations that mandate the provision of legal aid, shelter, or counseling to victims of SOGIESC-based hate crimes.

103.   Contributors from all analyzed countries reported that SOGIESC-based hate crimes are often not reported to law enforcement authorities owing to systemic barriers, including fears of revealing their SOGIESC status, lack of awareness about reporting mechanisms, fears that reporting will not result in any effective remedy, and lack of legal protections altogether.

2.   Recommendations

104.   Countries may consider adopting the following legal and policy practices to address SOGIESC-based hate crimes and to provide adequate support services to victims of hate crimes:

(i)   Enact laws and regulations that criminalize SOGIESC-based hate crimes and recognize these hate crimes as aggravated circumstances. Amend existing laws and regulations to extend protections to sexual and gender minorities.

(ii)   Institutionalize mechanisms for regular monitoring and reporting of SOGIESC-based hate crimes to facilitate effective investigation and remedy for hate crimes.

(iii)   Enact laws, regulations, and policies that mandate training and sensitization of law enforcement and judicial authorities to recognize SOGIESC-based hate crimes. Include training and sensitization of law enforcement and judicial authorities in national human rights plans.

(iv)   Provide legal assistance, safe shelters, and other support mechanisms to victims of SOGIESC hate crimes.

105.   Additionally, countries may adopt the following good practice to curb stigma and biases that promote SOGIEC-based hate crimes:

(i)   Implement public campaigns to increase awareness of protections against SOGIESC-based hate crimes and to address the stigmatization of LGBTI people.

Standardized Questionnaire

The following standardized questionnaire was sent to each country expert to collect details on relevant legislative and regulatory frameworks for each indicator set. The standardized questionnaire was developed jointly with the World Bank.

Indicator	Questions
Deciminalization of SOGI	
1.	Are there any laws, constitutional provisions, and/or regulations that criminalize people based on sexual orientation, gender identity and expression, and sex characteristics?
1.a	Sexual orientation?
1.b	Gender identity and expression?
1.c	Sex characteristics (intersex people)?
2.	Does your country criminalize same-sex relations between consenting adults?
3.	Is the legal age for consensual sex the same for heterosexuals as for sexual and gender minorities?
4.	Are sexual and gender minorities targeted with other laws such as on vagrancy, public nuisance, or public morals?
4.a	Sexual orientation?
4.b	Gender identity and expression?
4.c	Sex characteristics (intersex people)?
5.	Are there any laws and/or regulations that assign transgender and intersex people who have been convicted of a crime to be incarcerated in correctional departments, jails, and prisons based on their gender identity and expression and sex characteristics?
6.	Are there any laws and/or regulations that criminalize certain conduct (sex, sex work, needle-sharing, exposing officials, etc.) of people living with HIV?
7.	Are there laws and/or regulations that prohibit persons from freely expressing their gender expressions (e.g., laws against "crossdressing")?

continued on next page

Appendix *table continued*

Indicator	Questions
	Access to Education
1.	Are there any laws, constitutional provisions, and/or regulations that prohibit discrimination against students and/or teachers in educational settings based on sexual orientation, gender identity and expression, and sex characteristics?
1.a	Sexual orientation?
1.b	Gender identity and expression?
1.c	Sex characteristics (intersex people)?
2.	Are there any laws and/or regulations that prohibit discrimination in school admission based on SOGIESC?
2.a	Sexual orientation?
2.b	Gender identity and expression?
2.c	Sex characteristics (intersex people)?
3.	Are there any laws and/or regulations that prohibit bullying, cyberbullying, and harassment against students and/or teachers in the educational system that includes students based on actual or perceived SOGIESC?
3.a	Sexual orientation?
3.b	Gender identity and expression?
3.c	Sex characteristics (intersex people)?
4.	Are there any laws and/or regulations that mandate the revision of national textbooks/national curriculum in primary and secondary education to eliminate discriminatory language (homophobic, transphobic, or intersex-phobic language, for example) or by adding gender-inclusive and non-heteronormative language (such as "students" instead of "boys and girls" and "family" or "caring adult" instead of "mom and dad" and normalizing the use of pronouns, for example)?
5.	Are there any laws and/or regulations that mandate training of schoolteachers and other school staff in primary and secondary education on antidiscrimination of students who are sexual and gender minorities or have atypical sex characteristics (or intersex people), or those perceived as such?
6.	Are there any laws and/or regulations that mandate the creation of courses on sex education in a SOGIESC-inclusive manner in secondary and tertiary education?
7.	Are there any concrete mechanisms (national or local) for reporting cases of SOGIESC-related discrimination, violence, and bullying or cyberbullying toward students, including incidents perpetrated by representatives of the education sector such as teachers and other school staff?
8.	Are there laws and/or regulations that prohibit students dressing/expressing themselves in accordance with their gender identity?
9.	Are there any antidiscrimination laws and regulations ensuring that people living with HIV enjoy equal rights at schools?

continued on next page

Appendix *table continued*

Indicator	Questions
	Access to Labor Markets
1.	Are there any laws, constitutional provisions, or regulations prohibiting discrimination based on sexual orientation, gender identity and expression, and sex characteristics (SOGIESC) in public and private sector workplaces at the national level?
1.1	In the public sector?
1.1.a	Sexual Orientation?
1.1.b	Gender Identity and Expression?
1.1.c	Sex Characteristics (Intersex people)?
1.2	In the private sector?
1.2.a	Sexual Orientation?
1.2.b	Gender Identity and Expression?
1.2.c	Sex Characteristics (Intersex people)?
2.	Are there any laws and/or regulations prohibiting discrimination in recruitment in the public and private sector based on SOGIESC?
2.1	In the public sector?
2.1.a	Sexual Orientation?
2.1.b	Gender Identity and Expression?
2.1.c	Sex Characteristics (Intersex people)?
2.2	In the private sector?
2.2.a	Sexual Orientation?
2.2.b	Gender Identity and Expression?
2.2.c	Sex Characteristics (Intersex people)?
3.	Are there any laws and/or regulations prohibiting an employer from asking an individual's SOGIESC and/or marital status during the recruitment process?
3.a	Sexual Orientation?
3.b	Gender Identity and Expression?
3.c	Sex Characteristics (Intersex people)?
4.	Are there any laws, constitutional provisions and/or regulations prescribing equal remuneration for work of equal value for sexual and gender minorities?
4.a	Sexual Orientation?
4.b	Gender Identity and Expression?
4.c	Sex Characteristics (Intersex people)?

continued on next page

Appendix *table continued*

Indicator	Questions
	Access to Labor Markets
5.	Are there any laws and/or regulations prohibiting the dismissal of employees on basis of their perceived or actual SOGIESC?
5.a	Sexual Orientation?
5.b	Gender Identity and Expression?
5.c	Sex Characteristics (Intersex people)?
6.	Are there any laws and/or regulations that allow an employee to bring a claim for employment discrimination on SOGIESC grounds in the public and private sector?
6.1	In the public sector?
6.1.a	Sexual Orientation?
6.1.b	Gender Identity and Expression?
6.1.c	Sex Characteristics (Intersex people)?
6.2	In the private sector?
6.2.a	Sexual Orientation?
6.2.b	Gender Identity and Expression?
6.2.c	Sex Characteristics (Intersex people)?
7.	Is there a national equality body or national human rights institution with the explicit mandate to handle charges of employment discrimination related to SOGIESC?
7.a	Sexual Orientation?
7.b	Gender Identity and Expression?
7.c	Sex Characteristics (Intersex people)?
8.	Does the pension system provide the same benefits to same-sex partners provided to different-sex spouses?
8.1	In the public sector?
8.2	In the private sector?
9.	Does the law consider valid registered partnerships and/or civil unions entered into by same-sex partners in other countries?
10.	Does the law consider valid legal marriages entered into by same-sex partners in other countries?
11.	Are there any laws and/or regulations prohibiting discrimination against people living with HIV/AIDS in the workplace?
12.	Are there any laws and/or regulations that require workplaces to have inclusive facilities, such as gender-neutral toilets?
13.	Are there any laws and/or regulations that prohibit employees to dress/express themselves in accordance with their gender identities?
14.	Are there any laws and/or regulations that prohibit employers from asking employees for HIV tests?

continued on next page

Appendix *table continued*

Indicator	Questions
	Access to Public Services and Social Protection
1.	Are there any laws, constitutional provisions and/or regulations that prohibit discrimination based on sexual orientation, gender identity and expression, and sex characteristics in accessing any of the following services?
1.1	In health care?
1.1.a	Sexual Orientation?
1.1.b	Gender Identity and Expression?
1.1.c	Sex Characteristics (Intersex people)?
1.2	In housing?
1.2.a	Sexual Orientation?
1.2.b	Gender Identity and Expression?
1.2.c	Sex Characteristics (Intersex people)?
1.3	In unemployment benefits?
1.3a	Sexual Orientation?
1.3b	Gender Identity and Expression?
1.3c	Sex Characteristics?
1.4	In social security coverage for people with severe disability?
1.4a	Sexual Orientation?
1.4b	Gender Identity and Expression?
1.4c	Sex Characteristics?
1.5	In old age benefits/pensions for persons above statutory pensionable age?
1.5a	Sexual Orientation?
1.5b	Gender Identity and Expression?
1.5c	Sex Characteristics?
1.6	In social security programs for low-income families with children?
1.6a	Sexual Orientation?
1.6b	Gender Identity and Expression?
1.6c	Sex Characteristics?
1.7	In other services?
1.7.a	Sexual Orientation?
1.7.b	Gender Identity and Expression?
1.7.c	Sex Characteristics (Intersex people)?
2.	Does the public health insurance scheme provide equal benefits to same-sex partners as to different-sex partners?
3.	Does the national census include questions on the SOGIESC status of individuals?
3.a	Sexual Orientation?
3.b	Gender Identity and Expression?
3.c	Sex Characteristics (Intersex people)?
4.	Are civil society organizations related to (i) sexual minority rights, (ii) transgender rights, and (iii) intersex rights permitted under the law?
4.a	Sexual Orientation
4.b	Gender Identity and Expression
4.c	Sex Characteristics (Intersex people)

continued on next page

Appendix *table continued*

Indicator		Questions
		Access to Public Services and Social Protection
5.		If yes, are these organizations subject to limitation by the state on the basis of national security, public order, morality or other grounds?
	5.a	Sexual Orientation
	5.b	Gender Identity and Expression
	5.c	Sex Characteristics (Intersex people)
6.		Are there any laws and/or regulations that prohibit civil society organizations (CSOs) from providing social services specifically to sexual and gender minorities? (for example, vaccination, sanitation, transportation, family planning, health services (psychological, physiological and sexual and reproductive), HIV preventive services (for example, condoms, lubricants, pre-exposure prophylaxis, and so on), and information on vulnerable sexual practices, antiretrovirals, medication for gender-reassignment surgery, support for transgender people during/after gender reassignment surgery?)
	6.a	Sexual Orientation
	6.b	Gender Identity and Expression
	6.c	Sex Characteristics (Intersex people)
7.		Are there any laws and/or regulations imposing funding limitations on civil society organizations on the provision of such services?
	7.a	Sexual Orientation
	7.b	Gender Identity and Expression
	7.c	Sex Characteristics (Intersex People)
8.		Are there laws and/or regulations that establish National Human Rights institutions that include sexual orientation, gender identity, gender expression and sex characteristics (SOGIESC) within their mandate and/or specific institutions with an explicit mandate to advance the inclusion of people with diverse SOGIESC identities?
	8.a	Sexual Orientation
	8.b	Gender Identity and Expression
	8.c	Sex Characteristics (Intersex People)
9		Is there a national equality body or national human rights institution that handles charges of SOGIESC based discrimination in public services?
	9.a	Sexual Orientation
	9.b	Gender Identity and Expression
	9.c	Sex Characteristics (Intersex People)
10		When applying for a passport or ID cards, are there only two options for "male or female"?
	10.a	ID Card
	10.b	Passport
11.		Are there any laws and/or regulations that require the assigned sex on the passport and/or ID card to match the expression of one's gender?
12.		Are there any laws and/or regulations that allow an individual to obtain a new ID card or passport after gender reassignment?
13.		Are there any laws/regulations/policies that require health care officials to collect and report data on whether COVID-19 patients are sexual and/or gender minorities and people with sex characteristics variations/intersex status?
14.		Are there any laws and/or regulations that prevent sexual and gender minorities and people with sex characteristics variations/intersex status or same-sex partners from donating blood?
15.		Are there any legal or policy related limitations for sexual and gender minorities and people with sex characteristics variations/intersex status to accessing COVID-19-related Social Protection programs?

continued on next page

Appendix *table continued*

Indicator		Questions
		Civil and Political Inclusion
1.		Are there any members of Parliament or other national, elected representative body who openly self-identify as a sexual, gender minority or intersex?
2.		Are there any members of Cabinet or the executive branch that openly self-identify as a sexual, gender minority or intersex?
3.		Are there any members of the Supreme Court or other Highest Court that openly self-identify as a sexual, gender minority or intersex?
4.		Are there National Action Plans on SOGIESC?
	4.a	Sexual Orientation?
	4.b	Gender Identity and Expression?
	4.c	Sex Characteristics (Intersex people)?
5.		Are there any laws and/or regulations that restrict expression, civic participation, or association related to SOGIESC?
	5.a	Sexual Orientation?
	5.b	Gender Identity and Expression?
	5.c	Sex Characteristics (Intersex people)?
6.		Are there any centralized protocols for updating sex/gender in official certifications without pathologizing requirements?
7.		Can same-sex couples enter into a registered partnership or civil union?
8.		Can same-sex couples get legally married?
9.		Is second parent and/or joint adoption by same-sex partner(s) legally possible?
10.		Are there any laws and/or regulations that grant different-sex and same-sex couples equal access to assisted reproductive technology?
11.		Are there any laws and/or regulations that grant different sex and same-sex couples equal treatment regarding automatic co-parent recognition? (the same-sex partner of the parent who gives birth through medically assisted techniques should be automatically recognized as the second parent).
12.		Are there any laws and/or regulations that require gender-reassignment surgery for intersex children in order to receive a birth certificate?
13.		Are there any laws and/or regulations which provide protection to intersex persons (including children) against irreversible, non-emergency surgical or other medical interventions unless the intersex person has provided personal, free and fully informed consent?
14.		Are there any laws and/or regulations prohibiting/banning/protecting against the so-called SOGIESC "conversion therapy"?
15.		Are there any clinical classifications that categorize the following issues as a mental or physical disorder and/or pathologizes the following?
	15.a	Being Transgender
	15.b	Being Intersex
16.		Is there recognition of persecution based on SOGIESC as one of the grounds for asylum?
	16.a	Sexual Orientation?
	16.b	Gender Identity and Expression?
	16.c	Sex Characteristics (Intersex people)?
17.		Are there any laws, regulations or policies that restrict or prohibit movement due to COVID-19 based on gender?

continued on next page

Appendix *table continued*

Indicator	Questions
	Protection from Hate Crimes
1.	Are there any laws, constitutional provisions and/or regulations that criminalize hate crimes based on sexual orientation, gender identity, gender expression, and sex characteristics?
1.a	Sexual Orientation?
1.b	Gender Identity and Expression?
1.c	Sex Characteristics (Intersex people)?
2.	Are there any laws and/or regulations that require government agencies to collect data on hate crimes committed against sexual and gender minorities or those perceived to be sexual or gender minorities?
2.a	Sexual Orientation?
2.b	Gender Identity and Expression?
2.c	Sex Characteristics (Intersex people)?
3.	Are there mechanisms in your country for monitoring and reporting hate crimes against sexual and gender minorities?
3.a	Sexual Orientation?
3.b	Gender Identity and Expression?
3.c	Sex Characteristics (Intersex people)?
4.	Are crimes committed against someone based on that person's SOGIESC considered as aggravating circumstances by the law?
4.a	Sexual Orientation?
4.b	Gender Identity and Expression?
4.c	Sex Characteristics (Intersex people)?
5.	Are there any laws and/or regulations that mandate training of the following professionals on recognizing and identifying hate crimes? (for example, police officers, prosecutors, judges, social workers, and paramedics/doctors).
5.1	Police officers?
5.2	Prosecutors?
5.3	Judges?
5.4	Social workers?
5.5	Paramedics/Doctors?
5.6	Other?
6.	Are there any laws and/or regulations that mandate the provision of any of the following services to victims of hate crimes? (for example, legal assistance (including asylum applications and completing court forms), shelter/housing, forensic or medical examinations, and medical certificates).
6.1	Legal assistance (including asylum applications and completing court forms)?
6.2	Shelter/housing?
6.3	Forensics or medical examinations?
6.4	Medical certificates?
6.5	Other?
7.	What are the main reasons for not reporting incidents of SOGIESC discrimination in your country?

For indicator 7:

- Nothing would happen or change
- Not worth reporting it
- Did not want to reveal my sexual and/or gender identity
- Concerned that the incident would not have been taken seriously
- Didn't know how or where to report
- Too much trouble
- Dealt with the problem myself or friends
- Fear of intimidation by perpetrators
- Lack of legal protection and harassment or non-action by police
- Other reason: Please explain: